Nervous Arcs

&

The Body in Time

NERVOUS ARCS

Jordie Albiston

THE BODY IN TIME

Diane Fahey

Spinifex Press Pty Ltd,
504 Queensberry Street,
North Melbourne, Vic. 3051
Australia
spinifex@peg.apc.org

First published by Spinifex Press, 1995

Photograph of Jordie Albiston by Ian McBryde
Photograph of Diane Fahey by Jo Armour
Typeset in Goudy by Claire Warren
Cover design by Lin Tobias
Made and printed in Australia by Australian Print Group

National Library of Australia
Cataloguing-in-Publication entry:

Fahey, Diane.
    The body in time.

    ISBN 1 875559 37 X

    1. Australian poetry – 20th century. I. Albiston, Jordie,
    1961– . Nervous arcs. II. Title. III. Title: Nervous arcs.

A821.308

This publication is assisted by the Australia Council, the
Australian Government's arts funding and advisory body.

CONTENTS

Nervous Arcs

Jordie Albiston

About Jordie Albiston

Jordie Albiston has been writing for ten years and has had work published both in Australia and overseas. She was commended in the 1994 Premier's Poetry Award (Warana Writers Week) and received the Wesley Michel Wright National Poetry Prize in 1991. She has had her poetry read on a variety of radio programmes, has performed her work on international television and has been widely published in literary journals and magazines. She has just completed a PhD in literature, and has two children. She was born in, and lives in, Melbourne.

Acknowledgements

ædon
Blue Jacket (Japan)
bystander
Defined Providence (USA)
First Intensity (USA)
Going Down Swinging
Hecate
Imago
LiNQ
Mattoid
Meanjin
modern writing
Motherlode (Sybylla Feminist Press, forthcoming)
New Muse of Contempt (Canada)
Poems from the Rochester Castle
Poetrix
Second Degree Tampering (Sybylla Feminist Press)
The Café Review (USA)

"Rogue Art", public art program, The University
    of Melbourne (Victoria)
"Sambuca Blackboard Poems", Sambuca Café Bar
    (Victoria)
"Art on the MET" (Victoria)

"The Bottom Drawer", Radio 3PBS FM (Victoria)
"Writers at Work", Radio 3CR (Victoria)

Channel 19, Cambridge Cable Television (Boston)
Channel 31, SKA Television (Victoria)

"Whale Song" and "Grandmother" (part II) were awarded
the Wesley Michel Wright National Poetry Prize in 1991,
and "Emily Dickinson: A Modern Fascicle" was com-
mended in The Premier's Poetry Award for 1994 (Warana
Writers Week, Queensland).

Nervous Arcs

Contents

The Room

I am a woman locked in a
room in a house in a
suburb   you could call me

some kind of princess
though the only spinning
done is in my head   this is

my industry   I twirl a
gold thread of my own   I am
seated   back against door

awkward lotus   I work for
the good of the kingdom
look   the tapestries are torn

from the walls they lie in
heaps little piles of ash I
have cut them to bits I have

toiled for an age I have had
to destroy those centre
spreads   see on the floor

an eye a fringe a slice of
breast   my sour flesh   your
goddess is chopped to pieces

she is stacked on the floor
by my left knee   your queen
is in tatters   though your

madwoman is quite intact   it
is you who have divided
me   made me white as virgin

black as whore   golden as
any good mother   it is over
enough   I have forged

my own knife   any myth
pale offering   I will shred
watch out   I am weaving a

key on my quivering loom
I know my way out   I have
measured the depth of this

tower   this dungeon   my
room   I will burst free   no
phoenix no dragon but me

DROMANA SUMMER

(for my mother)

On the beach we are sitting
my mother and I   as the
others float   faraway
fisherpeople   high on the
ball of the bay.   We balance

the boat with green and
brown eyes   maintain the
hinge holding black dot to
deep blue   measure the
motion   the filial salinity

keep the sun stuck fast to
white sky.   Any moment
could suck them away.
The umbrella is spread like
an open mandarin   slices

of colour   a carnival wheel
spinning behind orange-lit
eyelids.   Our toes burrow
tunnels as we talk.   *Do you
think they are biting?   How*

*deep is that sea?   I wish
I could fly like a Pacific
Gull.*   All of a sudden   a
wave breaks   and frothy
tongues   five hundred of

them!   army of virgins
tiny brides   they impale
themselves at our feet.   *It
is the wash*   my mother
says.   She stands up slowly

and   leaving her book on
a terry-towelling mound
moves amongst shell piles
seaweedy breasts   towards
the shifting sea.   Shields

her vision.   Narrows her
eye.   Screws her breath
into a cat-gut line.   *The
Princess of Tasmania.*
Frill-edged hemispheres

lap at her shadow   her
feet press clouds through
the shining sand   and
standing at this lip like a
solitary tooth she gazes

at the place where the boat
should be.   Little insects
hang high above this scene
a distant squealing   a
horizontal humming   war

planes or seagulls circling
over her head until   *There
they are I can see them
now*   and lying beside me
my mother again   watches

the waves   *How they arch
and sparkle beneath this
cloud-carved vault!*   her
breathing and mine and that
of the now sleeping sea.

Whale Song

Cast off like a choirboy on the
celestial crescendo I ride my leviathan
through testaments of deep.   With my
good leg astern and my ivory bone
propped like a flag in the spiracle

of this beast I am Ahab still plowing
the vast body of then.   Three quarters
of me splutters in a fishbowl of water-
siege yet I am captain of this voyage
revenge my first mate, ancient memory

my faithful crew.   It is a teary expanse
that drenches my sight, eye of salt
lung of salt, my whole structure a tottery
pillar of fear-crusty salt.   Balanced
on the bulk between heaven and dismay

I sway, broken mast, mad harpoon, stuck
like a limpet on the hoary back of pain.
But do your worst, cetacean shadow
I have flukes of my own, and when you
sound I can hold breath for a lifetime.

Steeped in purpose precious as spermaceti
and morbid as ambergris, I am bound
in blubber no loving barb can frustrate.
Throw up what past treasure you can.
Blast me with your blowhole, I will not

jump ship until the sun itself drowns
and the moon becomes fish for I am one-
legged Ahab with no shore for my soul
only this ocean of opalescence to mirror
and mirror an old and landless heart.

SOLITARY BEACH

The whale supplies his own fuel and
burns by his own body.
It smells like the left wing of the day
of judgement.
— Herman Melville

My whale died within
on Solitary Beach
packed in salt
beneath a bleeding sky.

This is what I will say
when it is over.

The cord was caked
the spiracle dry
a jelly-quiver signalled
the final cry.

I will watch
until it is done.

I had no love to unstick
the jaw from the sand.
I had no love to unbeach
love.

No love is a swift harpoon.

He died within.
A silent death.
The gulls picked his soul
and flew it away.

God-speed I will say.

I sat on his back
to squeeze out the air.
I jumped and stamped
him flat.
I stared out his eye
till no eye was there.
I emptied my Jonah-belly
of life.

This is nobody's home.
Do not come back.

It is believed she will kill again.

I killed my whale
on Solitary Beach.
The flames keened a requiem.
Everything went.
The sea sucked itself
into a teardrop lament.
The cliffs closed in
on the scene.

This is how it will seem.

I bend my body
to a murderous shape.
I become one
with the immensity of death.
With my right hand
I light the infernal match.
With my left hand
I snuff out the sun.

EMILY DICKINSON:
A MODERN FASCICLE

I. Letter to Austin
. . . you must recollect that there are
two instead of one to be fed
& we have keen appetites over here . . .

I am starving   my mind turns
on tableaux of food   chestnuts
grapes   apples & cake   the
entertainment of the homesick
heart   My dear Brother Austin
I want to tell you   I declined to

visit the *bears* & monkeys   but
sat like a miser over his trove
eyeing his treasure   grinding
his gold   eating to quell this
Menagerie within   See   I have
devoured the gingerbread &

peaches   I am starving   red
pilgrims   the robin & I   Are
you not happy   I am so rapidly
gaining   correct ideas of female
propriety   Are you not pleased
with your bird-like sibling   I

peruse your words with the
sobriety of my station   sister
little sparrow   a chirp for a
life   highly accomplished
entirely overlooked   brilliant
as hunger   a cherry in my bite

II. *I like a look of Agony . . .*

Your white-lily mind advanced
through language as though
words were a European town
You devised the final solution

in cubic quatrains that rolled
the page flatter than Poland
or France   boots of lead in
your pretty head   a funeral

inside your brain   soldered
mouth and stapled breath   a
ceremonious procession of
death and destruction   low

feet staggering over the place
where bandaged souls lie and
goblins dance   like daisies
at Dachau   all in a row   It

was a formal war   The rack
enclosed you   fierce pricking
scimitars tickled your flesh
a weight with needles on the

pounds   a dainty mangling
a brutal song   your emphatic
thumb on the pleasure screw
heralding the history to come

III. *Dear* Susie

How dull our lives must seem
to the bride   and the plighted
maiden   We are two women

What can come of that!   We
have only the ruby to dine
upon   With the stealth of bees

we climb the back stairs   to
pluck pearls from the
clandestine rose   *Dear* Susie

never close   I am too far in
I hold your jewel in my hand
You are what I have feared

and desired   my cactus splits
her beard   Do not deny this
butterfly   Your loving Emily

IV. To T. W. Higginson c.1862
Are you too deeply occupied
to say if my Verse is alive?

And so once again   Sir
your gnome picks up
her pen   She is female
uneducated   small as
the wren   She seeks a
surgeon's instruction
She has invented a mere

handful of poesy   (six
hundred in all)   and
wonders if they breathe
or fall   or if they are
worthy then   Sir   you
call her gait ungainly
you say she lacks fair
control   Who is to be
her tribunal   when no
Monarch rules her soul?

V. Dickinson's Grave, July 27, 1993

EMILY DICKINSON
BORN   DECEMBER 10   1830
CALLED BACK   MAY 15   1886

It is raining in Amherst   I crouch
by your material remains   A cast-
iron balustrade stops you escaping
as if you were still alive   I am not
the first to huddle here   Scraps of

poetry litter the earth   a couple of
ribbons   one pink   one red   are
tied to the fancy coping   But today
there is only you and I   and sister
Lavinia lying nearby   to shiver in

the American rain   I picture you
pacing the secluded place   sewing
your bundles   securing a space in
this bustling language   scribbling
deliberately   Webster on lap   a

civil war going unnoticed   I see
the white heat of your solitary day
almost two thousand poems folded
away in hymnal subversion   your
private variorum   secret religion

of capitals   dashes   meter   and
rhyme   I sit by your grave now
leaning to hear   the form of your
lexicon   bolder than death   the
precise punctuation of your breath

UTERUS

Which artist would not wish to dwell
at the central organ of all motion . . .
                                        – Paul Klee

I have no point   to make
my womb is round   my
logic circuitous   I ache

in nervous arcs   One by
one   the children come
in a curve   out from my

pear-shaped part   I tithe
such lives in the belly
of this church   I writhe

behind the delphic door
woven from female hair
This sanctum is a store-

house of unspoken words
difficult languages under
the tongue   the hordes

fail to understand   With
silence as my guide   I
command them   to live

in uncomfortable ears
on modern laps   a chorus
of noisy loves and fears

proceeding from a uterine
mind   These are my off-
spring   This is the time

to conceive and deliver
the thin stream of syllables
into the serpentine river

MATER CARTA

I.

Amniotic apology
Flat on my stomach and
staring at you

dream-flipping slowly
your cells going off
like tiny bombs

Trying to talk
through sand-shoved gills
holding forth about this

your one
sorry swim
And me

frozen ocean
dry ice
too cold for you

and the strange
aquatic leap
Too cold for life

I know how to drown
sad secrets
rude fish

I know how to kill
and make
into white

the weak kick
the soft stroke
the sweet and dreadful breath

II.

Jaws may open
and caves
may close

but it's the body
of life
kills me

Obsequious uterus
reeling my reasons
like fish into fiction

its daily grand shanties
sharper than fins and
tentacle-thin

I want to walk on land
Show me an egg
I say cook it

Point to a sea
I say look
at the view

body of water
curious headland
something to think about

during a drought
the salt lip curled back
the stained ocean floor

impossible molluscs
dried into rock
and the sun-smart

land-stripping
sand-spitting
crowd

here for the blood-spill
dollar-filled bucket
picking at bits

of this wasteland
my belly
white-boned

clean-licked and
stuck to the
skeletal sky

Little more than remains
a hook-shaped attack
the stink of a life

fished dry
cruel gutted
thrown back

III.

Into my stomach
has dropped a
heart   all day

it has burned
there   stopped
in its orbit of

beating through
borders and
unlit blockades

Smoking meteor
smouldering
comet it flips

and flaps sick
fish in my
lap   I want it

to light up my
vein   again
make me recall

your blood in
my heart in your
body my blood

and rise like
a red sky
over our love

WHEN THE WOMAN WAS A GIRL

she arose in one body and stood on
symmetrical feet. The world
was measured in big-toes and hands
her hips spanned a bridge from
herself to herself   her spine was

a silent throne. When the woman
was a girl   she drew crosses for
plaits   called her shadow by name
and   reaching toward the stars
could touch. She lay among

nasturtiums at noon. The flowers
were yellow   jaffa-orange   red
she held the mustard-pea under her
tongue   stuck flat green leaves to
her thighs with saliva   placed

petals over her eyes. When the
woman was a girl   she picked
blackberries with her teeth. She
watched time drift past in shades of
blue   and sang with the magpies

at the sky. A bee stung her under
the lemon tree   teetered and died
when she suddenly cried   a fish
brushed her shin with its fins.
When the woman was a girl she

walked and ran and flew and swam
with all the other creatures. Flat
on her back in the nasturtium patch
she measured the world in big-toes
and hands   and it was very large.

ON FIRE

(for Patty, Malcolm and Robbie)

On fire, the old shed glows
like a fairytale castle or a
heart. The kids have come

in gumboots and dressing
gowns, drawn from their
dinners to see the display

of a childhood going up in
flames. This is the place
where we played. Straight

after school until hunger
or fear turned shed walls
to strangers and bad men

with bayonets running us
down, we made promises
like houses and lived there

for always, selling secrets
and stories escape routes
from time. Now it is all lit

up. With tightly shut eyes
we can see through the
red to the dark sky behind

broody as adolescence and
smelling like blood. There
is nothing to say. We return

to cold dinners, older than
adults, heavy with heat, the
grey ashes spiralling down.

FRIDA KAHLO: AN EXHIBITION

(for Trudy Clutterbok)

I. *Retablo*

The spear-head of steel was central
to both body and work. Penetrating
the back   left side   belly level   it
thrust its nose through your vagina
and nailed you   clever icon   to

art. You were no longer a virgin.
Denuded by the force of that holy
relic   showered with powdered
gold   *La bailarina! La bailarina!*
Alejandro placed your broken form

in the display window of a shop. You
screamed louder than the Red Cross
siren. Spinal column broken   three
places   lumbar region   collarbone
broken   third and fourth ribs   right

leg   eleven fractures   crushed right
foot   pelvis broken   three places
and the hand-rail of God   skewing
you to the future like a Mexico City
Christ. It was a strange collision you

said. In the hospital   at night   death
danced around your bed. Enclosed in
plaster   sarcophagus of science   you
dreamed of someone wailing and the
vivid colour red. You dreamed while

Matilde joked   got the whole ward
laughing   and when you closed your
eyes onto your own adolescent flesh
gold-spattered   blood-speckled   and
pierced with rusty fate   you dreamed

of completing that first picture. The
violence of tiny brush-strokes was no
panoply. Eighteen years old   you held
the image in your teeth and began the
painting   the unbroken coming back.

II. Love

Diego, come down.

Ugly forty-one-year-old
woman-chasing muralist
Mexican   prodigy
bohemian   radical

I have come to show you my painting.

Diego Rivera   fattened
on fame   Buddha-faced
frog prince   *jarabe-*
dancing   communist

I have a fine nervous body.

A year in Spain a brief
sojourn in Paris   A pal
to Picasso   Diaghilev
Apollinaire   Stein

I have long hair dark eyes a broken column.
I have brows like the wings of a blackbird.

Diego Rivera   love and
fascination   *tequila*
conversation   The
Elephant and the Dove

III. "What the Water Gave Me" (1938)

Bouyancy   Attitude   Brueghel
Bosch   A break from the grind
of gravity   The water got hotter
as I worked   at the thought of

memories glimpsed   sexuality
pain   death floating in circles
around my painted toes   The
same severed vein   life-blood

slick-drip   stringing image to
image in a paint-box of misfits
Volcano   Daddy long-legs   My
private collection   Sailing-boat

Tight-rope   Self-portrait with
strangled woman   A thin wash
over everything   A comment
from Breton   I never knew I

was a surrealist   until the bus
I was riding   the *balero* in my
hand   a haemorrhage of pretty
colours   a palette for an eye!

IV. Death

I am the Aztec *Tehuana* on the silent
wall   upright Doric princess in a
miniature frame   Frida the gimp
from the city of Coyotes   Frida the
peg leg with a little clay deer   I am

the broken-winged one-legged doll
of *alegría*   Cracked at the chest
Fungus for a foot   Arrows to pin-
point the places of pain   What
tragedy?   They are going to cut off

my *pata*   So what?   I am heroic
spectacular   tied to my chair   I
paint the embrace of life by light
Bring me my boots   luxurious red
leather   Chinese gold trim   little

bells for joy   Inject! Inject!   I will
dance for my friends   in the sun
down below   the surface of the earth
where everything is backward   a
black angel rising   the dead having

a fling   a silver anniversary   a
solid gold ring   two litres of cognac
a thousand vials of Demerol   a man
in a *sombrero* stoking the kiln   I
am the *Tehuana* princess   my hands

on my breast   come closer Diego
I am beautiful in death   my face
is a festive wax skull   It was an
enormous exit I went through   my
love   an enormous and silent exit

KÜNSTLERROMAN

(for Robert Alder)

I first met you on a shore
where three lonely trees
divided the frame of your
gaze.   The ocean mass fell

over middle-distant reef
advanced like a wedding
march   steppes of white
lace   bride-limping out

of the Possession Island
embrace to collapse like
a girl on the sand.   You
did not know I was there.

Your hidden eye charted
the form of the place and
painted its face in yellows
and greys   land and sky

and sea and dream   the
whole world caught in a
canvas scheme   uniform
solid   almost touchable.

There were other scenes
too: Páros Bay mountains
forming a bowl to hold
the molten Greek sea

a man on a balcony   the
curve of a road   a lapful
of daisies   some boats.
With that rosary   your

palette   to embroider my
way   I stumbled over
prayers   in olive groves
on hillsides   followed the

fine trail of your painterly
pain   until landing on my
knees in a blood-spattered
poppy field   violent   war-

like   dangerously bright
I began to see   that seeing
is not simple   and memory
never slight   that the

boyhood spent darkly seeks
a life in the light   and that
colour   clever harlequin
is innocent   only at night.

BLACK IRIS III

I.

Outside the clinic trams rush
by   the rush-hour crowd

heaves along Bourke Street
It's cancer he says and looks

at me for the first time   I
hold the fact   examine its

weight and shape   roll it in
the palm of my hand   I drive

slowly home this other body
this stand-in version of me

II.

In the bathroom a woman glances
too quick   The mirror knows and
says   *It's a fact*   Suddenly she
looks unwell   *And so* (she scolds

her crêped belly) *did you lie?   We
had a deal   happiness for health
We had things to do   and now this
Don't think I believe in betrayal*

III.

I wake to the night   It is around me
and through me   I clutch my belly
of tar   black spider   It breathes of

death   wielding fronds   fat legs
through unforgiving flesh   I raise
the axe   *not me not me!*   and drop

it through the creeping thing   Cell
of corrosion   Malignant arachnid
Battery of organised dark   I locate

the threat within each chamber
and cut it out   Somewhere inside
a nerve slowly opens like a heart

IV.

Georgia O'Keeffe   *Black Iris III*
Petaloid tunnel folding pink mauve

and tentative grey   a couple of
moth wings   still wet   I breathe

and breathe   banish science from
the air   beckon health   *A Black*

Bird with Snow-covered Red Hills
The Lawrence Tree   Music - Pink

and Blue II   I scent a fragrance
somewhat sweeter than death   sense

spider become orchid   and illness
a field of red-riddled poppies   I

place my hands on luminous flesh
settle for the calm   string hope

like a daisy-chain round and around
this   burgled body   my home

SURFACES

The surface is where most of the action is.
The surface is what touches the animal...
                                    – J. J. Gibson

We see from the outside
the felt-like integument
stretched over the inner
mound. This parchment
of skin is written across

and again by fingers and
fabric   water and air
the chirographic events
of the day. We hold in
our hands the circular

interstice   elastic cell-
nucleus   we tongue the
wet blueish food. *This
is the breast*   we say.
In memory and movies

on sad toilet walls   in
medical diagrams public
house diatribes   *This
is the female breast.* The
instinctive infantile cry

defines the protuberance
mamma. A medieval
doctor   fame-famished
hungry   discovers the
mammary gland. *Pink-*

tipped   nipple-shaped
milk-secreting papilla
fatty tissue   fibrous
tissue   the lactiferous
ducts. He is a believer

in love. We print his
description in clinical
texts and suck with our
minds   pornography
anatomy   a reservoir

of signs   holding our
secret close to the chest
mouthing the mystery
drawing the line. *This*
we say   *is the breast*.

CANCER IN JUNE

(for Helen Polak)

I.

I expected to be a stranger in
the room of your dying   no match
for the charts   the clinical hush
the step   the starch   the skilful
hearts of your new unchosen

companions. I had been warned
of the speed of your decay.
You did the talking   my language
betrayed   by the silences hiding
between murmured Latin codes

and the secret of your pain
the plain lack of logic in this thing
at your age   the industry of the
illness   the severity of the phage
eroding carefully   abstracting

your life   forming   re-forming
buying your rights   the zodiac
of hospitals   the false colour
white. *I don't want to close my
eyes*   you said   *the clouds*

the smog   the colours at night
you speaking to me dreamily of
*cars on Punt Road   the reflected
lights   yellows and greys   nice
nurses   good times   your*

morphine voice   your eyes. I
listened to everything   you could
see from both sides   and
learned from your body
the shameless grace of a breath.

This is so stupid   you said as I left
but cancer is not stupid   no
cancer is clever   knowing just
when to open its many mouths and
just who to taste with its tongues.

II.

Winter. A cold wind.
Dark horizons.
The slow gathering

of ice. Couldn't you
feel it inside?
Didn't your dreams

relay reports
from those cells
on the frontline

send for replacements
(molecular strategies)
punctuate your sleep

with dot and dash
breaths   unscramble
the code   sound out

the alarm
blow medical terms
down the streets

of your town
didn't
your body feel it?

How can it grow
grey secret   dull
enemy   year after

year   an army of
millions   advancing
malignant   and you

not know?
When does a cough
become cancer

and the lung
surrender   its
breathing its

breathing
for the black-coated
gasp   how does it

happen   this burning
this sermon
of mud

is it luck   is it
war   a decade of
maybe   unfortunate

blood   cigarettes
stress   is it
love?

III.

Two Helens captured in black
and white gowns   polarised
portraits I carry around with
me   conflicting pictographs

binary ideograms   campus or
cancer ward   jostling my sight
A photograph propped by the
sick woman's bed   just on a

year ago   smiling and holding
a rolled-up degree   and Helen
in hospital   a snapshot disease
the negative picture   cellular

striptease   X-ray   irradiation
still life with dead trees   The
visual dispute   the fight in my
eye   Helen in hospital   Helen

alive   a cruel clash of images
cinema of disguise   You lying
there finally   learning to die
A short course in cancer   a

career in last breaths   this
clinic your college   this bed
your desk   Helen in hospital
A winter graduation in death

PURITAN

Three syllables strong you
called me Pequot at Mystic
fired wigwams to the ground
in a sacrament of slaughter.

Dreaming old testament
you were David and Jehu
you were Luther at Münster
and the externall burning of

Rome. You could not quite
kill me enough. Received and
entertained at the point of
your sword I did not want to

die. The semantics of holy
genocide brave rhetoric of
love what a wondrous man
you all were. Word sperm

pure. New World spirituall.
Orgasm. Iconoclasm. Deity
divine. You prayed as you
came. Prayed as you called

me Hutchinson whore cursèd
devill antinomian 1637 called
me woman. I heard glory cry
from Boston to Revelation

that filthie Sinne   the Indian
the female   chiming from
steeples an orgy of fear
erect unforgiving and who

have we here? We must
throw Jezebel down. God
works in strange ways you
must understand. (*So they*

threw her down. And they
found no more of her than
the skull, and the feet, and
the palms of her hands.)

THE SALEM PAPERS, 1692

I. Examination of Martha Carrier

Abigail Williams w'o hurts you?
Goody Carrier of Andover.
Eliz. Hubbard who hurts you?
Goody Carrier.

He is speaking while they
reel and writhe. The
court room looks like a
fair. Ann Putnam cries of

a pricking pin. If I had a
pin I would stick it in. He
is speaking quickly his
soul on fire his words are

branding irons. He asks
can I but look at them
and not knock them down.
I watch his face I keep my

place and say: They will
dissemble then. Susannah
Sheldon in a trance: *I*
wonder could you murder?

I could not kill until this
day the devil in these
girls. And Mary Walcott
testifies: *she killed ten no*

twelve thirteen! No one
hears I tell the truth. I
speak they don't believe.
Mercy Lewis in a fit. Now

there's a name I will not
cry: *oh Mercy Mercy on*
my life falling howling
inventing sin. I will never

let you in. Just take me
to the other place (The
devil girls are tortured
great. There is nought to

do) but bind me fast.
Hand to foot to common
heart. And let all evil
slowly freeze this court

this crowd these winter
trees. (Bound hand and
foot.) I hope they sleep. I
hope they get their ease.

There goes Goody Carrier.
She bites me pinches
me presses my throat.
There goes Goody Carrier.

II. Examination of Abigail Hobbs

I will speak the truth. I have seen
sights and have been scared. Have

seen dogs and many creatures. In
the woods. In the day. Something

like a man. It was at the Eastward.
3 years agoe. It was at Casko-bay.

He said he'd give me fine things if
I'd do what he did say. At our house.

Like a cat. I saw things like men.
They would give me fine clothes

if I did fine things for them. No
I did not. Yes I did. I mean the

Devil. Like a man. A black man
with an hat. No. Yes. I cannot

tell. I speak the truth and speak
it well. Hear him whisper in my

ear his pretty Abigail is here. I
cannot hear now what you say.

(The examinant then taken DEAF
the Court ordered her away.)

III. Examination of Martha Corey

You are now in the hands of Authority.
Tell us here why you hurt these girls.

(*I do not*)

Just answer the questions put to you.
Why do you afflict these poor souls?

(I am innocent)

That's not the answer we want from you.
We ask the questions. You answer true.

(Pray let me pray)

We do not send for you to pray. But give
us what we ask of you. Why do you

(I do not)

What? Her Majestie's Court needs to
know. Answer so the record will show
what is your book? who is your God?
confess to Jehovah up on high tell us
where and when and what and why

(Because I am a Woman

IV. Examination of Candy

now i see nothin but
black book eyes   one
bout death an one
bout lies   there is no
choice i got no voice
What black man is that?

see no black man but
you   white man   hat
on head and book in
hand   that make me
witch in this fine land
Candy! are you a witch?

me no witch in candy
land   candy mother
no witch   candy good
barbados land   candy
mistress give   *Which*
woman is witch?   you

got book you know
what right   i write my
name i make my mark
she make me scrub till
gorgeous white an   *Is*
Candy black?   black

an white an white an
black   i wash an cook
till all thing bright   i
wash the pot an light
the   *Black man in your*
bed at night?   candy

black no say no more
she pull my head i
see the floor   i miss
my man   *The bad*
black man?   i miss
my man give candy

love   *You sign your*
name?   give candy
love   *You witch?*
me good   *We bring the*
tree   you bring black
man to marry me

V. Gallows Hill

That upon fryday next
between the houres of Eight and twelve
the s'd witch be hanged by the neck
untill she be de[ad]

Climbing their ladder
up into song it's a thing
strong as wood my feet
tread. I can see my home

from up here. Cows in the
pasture hogs in the yard
they come in one silent
throng. I hope someone

remembers *Hickety*
Pickety my black hen I
hope someone remembers
something from wrong

my swing on this bough
Hush-a-bye baby on the
tree top my *Hey diddle*
diddle to Father and King

there *is the steeple here*
is the rope I hope someone
remembers me *Ride away*
ride away Sarah shall

hope that I satisfy hope
that I sing *Here sits the*
Lord Mayor here his two
men the Lord's Prayer

badly snap of my bone
Heaven accept me here I
run in *Chin-chopper chin-*
chopper chin-chopper chin

AFTER THE HANGINGS

After the hangings there is
something like peace. The branch
resumes its natural bend   the
heart becomes human   the finger

returns to its hand. Soon after
the hangings   friends drop over
the dollar recovers   the shovel
is suddenly dry. We recite the

future with wit and precision
pleased to be chosen   glad it is we
who have somehow survived.
The air breathes more cheaply

we sleep without grief   our
dreams slowly curling like feathers
or leaves into song   it was it was
never we who were wrong.

Opening and closing our hearts
on that bough   how good
to know our sin goes with the
dark   before the new day's start.

BONE

A slip of skin contains
it   a branch of vein
a fancy muscle wound

around in ivy coils
conceals it like a ruin
A bruise of lavender

lilac wisteria blooms
blue flower   cluster
of grapes to mark the

moment of impact
The bone is beautifully
broken   If tendrils

of pain unfurled inside
you opening slowly I
will never know   the

garden secret   interior
almanac   will only
recall the sign on your

flesh   that final floral
emblem   freshly-laid
wreath   admire the

design   and wonder
did it fade in the quiet
season of your death

GRANDMOTHER

I.

Two books of Beethoven piano sonatas
black and covered with silk   prizes
you won before your hands curled like
resolute foetuses back upon themselves

I see you play   dark eyes penetrating
a pale papered surface of hieroglyphic
significance   difficult to decipher
through decades of silence and harder

to hear than an old woman's more or
less audible sigh   You drag your
school satchel down very same streets
you swish your Victorian wedding

gown   and groan with the delivery of
your daughter   my mother   the only
child you will push into the day   We
share things you would never dare

mention   I want to tell   the abortion
the divorce   but tight-lipped you close
quietly those quaint inner doors   laced
with morality and hinged on Christian

lore   You do not want to hear   I
watch you weigh medicine tradition
religion with love   and choose   love
I place your photo against the faded

Moonlight Sonata and play poorly this
favourite   your arthritic smile as
sweet as barley sugar   your young-
girl ears straining from the hospital

bed   I flex my fingers   clench them
into stiff-jointed balls as you grasp
rosewood cane   stainless steel frame
and tiptoe gently   out the back door

II.

Placing my neat brown foot beside
your twisted toes nothing divides
us but half an old century   You
marvel at my beauty   I wince
at your great age   If I were you
I would just get up   and walk

You are my study I watch closely
through years   the deliberation
of pain   the mute channeling of
deformity into that place   where
body is not bent thing   but space
the ballerina mind can wander in

When I was your age I looked like
you   I search your face for my
own future   crooked and etched
with brave decline   Is there no
system   no jar to preserve life-
impulse in bottles of pretty and

young?   You chide my fear with
antique jewels   *The beauty within*
If eyebrows were meant to be
plucked et cetera   I fold into shame
more ugly than wrinkles and begin
to see you truly free   winging

your way through portentous tenets
that bind me tighter than any
disease   This is it   I am twisted
and taut beneath severe ideals   my
neat brown foot not quite so neat
my beauty more untrue than true

I dethrone the mirror within my
head   and hang instead a picture of
you   younger and more ancient than
the silk rope of years   You may hang
there forever   first lady and cover
girl   mother of mother of mine

III.

she is going now   to meet her
love   and the man who sells crays
at ten and six a pound   she is
going quietly   dressed in church

best   is my collar straight my
hair too flat   I arrange pink
nightgown   lightly kiss grey curls
you look beautiful I say   she says

take me to church   which way
to that place where angels sing and
age is the twinkle in each new
thing   I have no science no map

to clasp the worn crooked fact
no theory no recipe no methodist
hymn   I bend down close
place lips against cheek   it is

always Sunday now   take me to
church   what to say   turn
shiny wheelchair   silent silver
chariot   into hospital corridor

glide over linoleum with plastic
faith   here is the church here
is the steeple   the trolley of
instruments table of communion

piped music the litany   a devout
congregation behind each door
hear the man   he is calling
me   crays   crays ten and six a

pound   she is going to meet him
dressed in her best   no hospital
here   only the church I don't see
and god the one with the crays

WINDOW

(for Ian McBryde)

I saw right in when you
opened   the carefully
set table the scar on the

hill the drum still beating
like a heart   It was quiet
in there   you moved

without sound   I watched
you fly the white sky
your home   I watched you

die mid-flight   Then
waking like winter to the
purity of season your hand

closed like a trigger over
love   The unfurling
fingers were braver than

flags   the pale palm
curled into mine   I saw
right in when you opened

the rifle empty   the
animals asleep   snow lying
like a baby over pain

WANTING BEETHOVEN

(for my father)

I. Exposition

It is so loud in there
sometimes and then
sometimes so quiet:
a thin thread of aria

over flat water. Once
you were drowning I
cried Take me with
you. I wanted to go

I wanted to feel the
wet cadence over a
toe   the two tonnes
per string   pulling

at my hair. I wanted
the polyphonic tide
right up inside   my
brain   a sonata

the clunking of keys
a black piano thrown
down the stairs of
my soul. I wanted

to know your mind.
My cacophonous
heart knows little
of harmony   less of

the stress between
discord and song.
Still I long for the
tonic   the still note

of home   the sound
of the symphony
washing me whiter
than sand over stone.

II. Development

I know you are deaf
I can hear it from
here your head on

the keys when you
play *pianissimo*
the wooden frame

breaking when you
make your loss
loud. I sit with the

crowd my body in
my throat your
pain up my spine

the cadenza a kite
string I clutch with
both thighs. I am

not frightened of
romantic heights
but hope I land

somewhere on
classical ground
the pounding of

pianos guiding me
down: the ear of
the Emperor able

to hear the music
a certainty the
fact of the sound.

III. Recapitulation

It is so loud in there and
then so quiet   I feel you
drowning into the depths
and want to go too   the
suck of the solo the pull

of the tide   Yes I want
you inside   the edge of
allegro the lull of *legato*
arpeggio adagio encore
arrangement   invention

fantastico   your music in
mine   I bend my ear to
the clarity of water and
think I can hear   two
hearts sign in contrapuntal

display   yours an ocean
of orchestras churning
symphonies   semitones
waves of wet sound   and
mine the long dive down

IV. Coda

Now it is over. This
concerto you built
us to keep out the
noise this house of

hieroglyphics with
silence for windows
and dog stars for
doors. The circus is

coming with tickets
and televisions and
postcards and maps
they want you back:

in their arms a lost
lover in their eyes a
small sum hide your
head here they come

they have peanuts
and guns fold the
unfinished tenth
in your manuscript

mind climb inside
the piano take off
out of here and ride
forte into the sky.

BROWN BAG RAG

I bought the brown bag so it
must be mine. All day I have
been packing unpacking have
been packing my things in. It

holds quite a lot although not
what I thought I might need:
a page a pen (these things tend
to fit in) a flower a flute a red

pair of. The bag on the bed is
mine. I bought it because and
the man in the shop never said
Stop only Don't forget your

brown bag. I bought it today
and Hey have you ever packed
inside away it has zippers and
pockets and a place for every

and look at the exquisite brass
clasp. Exactly I thought when
I bought it. But then a phrase
of desire the scent of a thigh a

fingertip touching a cello with
Bach. Such items are hard to.
It is not very large. If I curl
up and. Maybe like. How does

one fold into a small space in
time? I bought what I thought
would I bought a brown bag.
Brought it back and started to

pack to stack my self in was
surprised by my very size. I
think a bit will somehow fit.
The rest will somehow arrive.

Three Short Pieces for Flute

I. *molto espressivo*

Into the instrument the
thing of itself the paper
the famous black marks

Through the facility and
evenness of fingering
the dynamics of *vibrato*

and tone   there is no
one in there but Ibert
The arching of fingers

my fingers   The belief
in breathing complete as
the phrase   The mind

my mind   allowing his
Pièce pour flûte seule
to unfold escape from

the script   an isolated
flag a waving of sound
a lonely roaming of air

II. *alla militare*

Always he stands there
settled on bookcase and
rising to ceiling in one
silver note of what can
not be sung   I know

the theme   cold practice
of penance or music   an
ornament   an instrument
of baptism   a chime   I
want him behind bars of

silence   Along with the
gasp *soffocato*   the
breath   I fall against
walls only want to be air
for this   last grasp at

harmony   dragging
my lungs like a net over
melody   my neck a
steel register my throat
a cylindrical drum

III. *sdegnoso*

Eighty per cent practice
time twenty per cent
performance   (I just
want to hear what it

sounds like)   It sounds
like a breath someone
left on a window an
embouchure open a cry

from a lung   it sounds
like Debussy has gone
(If I open my eyes can I
touch it)   silver-plated

body   cold head in my
hand   a call from *Die
Moldau*   a dirge
(Can you play something

dolce today)   *Il Flauto
Traverso   La Flûte
Travaille*   muted inside
me   a memory   a

Mass   the marching of
metal   the toll of a
dead-bell   the toneless
flutter of a tongue

EULOGY

Beginning with that first invisible
seed   the branches descend from
this upside-down tree in ink-lines
that represent blood. Priests and

professors people the page   each
name a life   each line a fact
molecular proof of the procreative
act   the familial sign of our cell

throughout time   a pyramidal
reminder   a clan. You were the
grand ninety-seven-year-old sire
a patriarch of sorts   born when

horses pulled trams along streets
and world wars had not been
invented. You were seventeen
when the first was declared. With

your veterinary degree still fresh
in your hand   you sailed to meet
those fleet-footed beasts   hauling
troops and artillery instead of trams

in Belgium England and France.
Caught between countries when
the Armistice was signed   six
weeks in Sydney with the Spanish

flu   you told tales of animals
braver than soldiers   wrote books
and painted   played Mozart by
ear   identified ships by their call

over water   thirty-two of my
years always contained you   until
now   you   sleeping at last   and
me   no longer a granddaughter.

A Nice Afternoon

It's a nice afternoon so I'm
taking a stroll   holding my
head high breathing it in.

Taking a stroll   3 o'clock's
a safe time for a woman
to walk   eighty per cent sure

she can stroll without more
than a billboard or wolf-
whistle to spoil it all with.

Warm sun pleasant breeze
I am stepping with ease the
white path 3 o'clock on a

nice afternoon. Blue sky
pink jasmine leans over a
fence   lending its scent to

the path I tread through
this my city   trying not to
notice pictures of women

the odd horn honking its
dread in my ear. Bracing my
self against swift bursts

of image and cat call I
stroll in safety past news-
stand   advertisement

hoping such strategies keep
somebody warm. On a nice
afternoon in the 3 o'clock

sun   women in bras on
fifty-foot screens   I am
trying to feel spring on a

nice afternoon   strolling
along in singlet and jeans
spying the idea through

unmade-up eyes   trying
not to hear   loud men in
slow cars. I am starting

to go cold as I stroll more
quickly   trying to stay
warm on a nice afternoon

under pictures of violence
and offers of lifts   they
want me to ride with them

high as the sky and pouting
like women in pictures they
buy   I am strolling more

quickly and trying not to
cry as I stroll   3 o'clock
on this nice afternoon

I am strolling and trying
hard not to scream That's
Not Me On The Screen on

a nice afternoon   cold and
alone   strolling the path
quickly   all the way home.

SUSANNA AND THE ELDERS

Deep in the apocryphal garden
you walk   at the same time
every day. You are difficult to
see through the foliage of
history   from where I am hid

beneath hard metallic bower
and kinetic sky   in the synthetic
arbour to come. Wife of Joakim
daughter of Helkias   your
beauty filters   through mastic

and holm leaf   your two maids
absent   your body in light   as
you wash your fair limbs at
noon. The people are departed
there is only you   and I   and

the new elders crouched behind
cameras and car wheels   eyeing
the feminine   spying the act
watching me always   watching
you. What is it you say as the

water encloses   what words
do you have for your hereafter
sister   caught in the stare-net
of modern men who want what
they see for a similar song? *Oh*

I am straitened   on every side
for if I do this thing   it is
death unto me   and if I do it
not   I land in their hands!
Two thousand years later   in

bedrooms   on bitumen   I
banish the elders to the splash
of your murmuring words:
Bring me oil and washing balls
and shut the garden doors.

RAPE SCENE

(for M.S.)

It was the same act   old rerun.
A little boring to the viewer perhaps
even the hero stifles a yawn   but
it was my first time   opening night
I could barely stammer my lines.

The stage was set: suburban night naked
woman in bed man forces lock children
shift in sleep.   I heard the cue
pretended to dream.
The script called for sweat   I sweated.

My doorway filled with shape just like I
knew it would.   I watched the shape
circle   unzip   just like I thought
it would   and you know and you
know when he breathed my air and strode

my bed bruised my flesh my silence my
home   my mind   just went   blank.
Stage-fright.
I forgot   the lot   oh what
what did I say on the news in the paper the

report?   Did I scream yell weep submit did I
survive?   Did somebody prompt a response
from inside?   I recall nothing
but darkly beneath the stage   the burn
of the audience   my children awake.

We were mute   divided by the
footlights of reality.   They gazed
(sweet innocents)   I closed my eyes   my
self.   I was not right for this part   never
was much of an actress   anyway.

NURSERY CRIME

(for Karen)

I do not wake to you
at night you black hat
stand you trenchcoat
man you softly slowly
fright   I shut my
eyes upon your hand
and jam your fingers
tight   you over
you under you have
no right I onto you
turn on the light the
threat the throat the
dark delight   you
bad you smack you
don't come back   I
tell I yell I spill the
beans you mad you
mean you not this
dream   I hit you
hurt I kick I slap you
name you game you
dripping lap   you
sad you said you Hey
let's play   I take
you naked make you
pray you fear you
dread I kill you dead

THE TREMBLING

Takes more to make me tremble
than war zones and newsreels
Kim Phuc running the napalmed
start. It takes more than the evil
root in the belly, the genderless baby
the foot in the heart to make me
tremble. Takes more than that
be surprised how much more, to get
me trembling at doorway atrocities
the burden of maleness, disposable
innocence, the limbless, the hard.
Lies do not tremble me, the reptilian
tongue, the rupture of hopeful, the
scream of the dumb. I do not
tremble at boots on bitumen, at the
feather in clay, the obsidian eye
I do not. Tremble. Trembling
remembers. The subway soliloquy.
The shut-down computer. Cars
tuned to parthenogenesis for a
mechanical god. I do not remember
the man in the movie, the blood
on the bucket, the street full of
signatures, the ten-dollar child.
Takes more than murder, the
fist-filled reception, the love poem
grieving, the first drug deceiving
the last foetus squealing, to
make me remember. What I do not.
Remember. Each thing that happens
each tiny event, scrubbing at
detail, detergent, reject, the mind

of remind, the beast in the bush
sleeping at last, the remembered
tremble of forget.

I, PRONOUN

I, the ninth letter and third vowel of the
Roman alphabet, going back through the
Greek *Iota* to the Semitic *Yod*, represents
a consonant (= English y as in *yearning*,
youth, etc.); in its original sense, we can
thereby surmise that I is equal to why,
which being the initial consonant and
question of you, yourself (as person,
pronoun, ex-lover) only goes to show
that we share a connection after all. You,
used with no definite meaning as indirect
object, or (better) qualified by a preceding
adjective (as in *cruel*, *uncaring*) and I, as
substantive, or *metaphorically* the subject
or object of self-consciousness, no longer
adhere to such a connection. For I, being
connective or quasi-connective, L. -*i*-
being the stem-vowel, as in *beaut-i-ful*,
or a weakened representative thereof, as
in *carn-i-vorous*, can no longer vow that
forming plurals of Y(ou) and I, as in the
phrase *yours faithfully*, is possible. I, as a
pronoun by which I denote myself, in the
nominative case, am not to be henceforth
referred to as half or any part therein of
the word *us*, a term no longer in use.
Examples in English of such grammatical
independence could be *I am alone*, or a
strengthened representative thereof, as in
I am strong. Any deviations of the oblique
cases of the singular outlined above can
only lead to misuse and abuse of I, as in
me.

ANOREXIA: AN ETYMOLOGY

I. A Body of Language

I close my mouth and
open my matter

denial my dictionary
starvation my syntax

western culture the con
text you place me in

This time it is your turn to
chew it over

the false obscenity
the female fact

my sentence your science
my discourse your danger

my vocab the vortex you
find your self in

I await the debate
the articulate exchange

the bone of contention
the body of ideas

food for thought
not just desserts

let us have our conversation
and eat it too

Put your ear right here
fit your eye

weigh your principles
choose your words

This time there are more
languages than yours

II. A Patient Discourse

Hunger is the industry she
employs her self in   honing
her form   reducing her
line   endeavouring to fit in
to this story   Her throat

opens and closes on nothing
now   She has become self-
sufficient has evolved her
self   belief in absence her
vanishing point   refusal

of nourishment   her food
Her breasts have learned to
be brave in their loss   her
belly has taught itself love
Her lips have begun to meet

over air   her arms have
turned themselves in   for
the hold   old answer
for everything   Where are
your hospitals now?   your

media   therapists   special
clinicians?   She is further
than you her body untouched
by logic   statistics   medical
remorse   Now she is flying

far above science   winging
her way to the other light
She sees you crowd in press
buttons   pull bells   your
tears the ocean that never got

wet   She sees you fill forms
go home to your meals   her
vision the memory you
speed into night   her body
the angel you never forget

III. Etymological Excerpts

An anorexic body (a retort,
with some reference to
spirit) refuses to swallow

(accept without opposition
or protest) the food
(a unique formation) of the

dominant culture (the
condition of being
thus trained). It chooses

the site of hunger
(often personified) as its
stated desire (a wish

as expressed) to avoid
the gaining of weight
(the force of an onslaught

or encounter in the field;
pressure exerted by
numbers). What it does

eat (feed destructively
upon) it proceeds to
vomit (give vent to or

utter abusive/objectionable
language) from its
depths. The dedicated

commitment to thus fast
(as an expression of
grief) transforms a

female body into one
which is extremely thin
(having relatively little

extension between opposite
surfaces).
An anorexic body chooses

death (deprivation of civil
life) over life
(the continuation of a

batsman's innings after a
chance of getting him out
has been missed), shifting

the arena of struggle
for control from the socio-
intellectual, where the

most anxiety (strained or
solicitous desire) is felt,
to the flesh.

IV. Newspaper Reportage

Picture the spectacle: *Juiceless ribs.*
Coat-hanger shoulders. Sunken
eyes. The newspaper never lies.

It feeds on clinical description
with relish   rewriting moments
in the collective story of the

grotesque (female) other. *Sally's*
teeth were slowly rotting away
her eyes were bulbous puffy slits

and her knuckles calloused and
scarred. Does it make you sick?
After meals she would plunge

her fingers her whole trembling
hand down her throat to vomit
the ugly calories away. *Bizarre.*

Red rims. Certain lines. Leaves a
legacy. We can spot a you know
what a mile off. Run the story.

Public interest. Next to the diet
page the quiz on thin thighs the
survey Must Love Be Fattening?

The newspaper never lies. We turn
to the page my god just imagine.
Can't believe she is. Wish we could

be. How does she do. It can't be
true. Such strategies betray a fear
of the flesh   a real living woman

starving on fetish. We hate you
we own you ninety cents with the
rest. We want you to close like

the sports page the funnies. We
want you to un-exist. The fact
that she is seen as a negative an

absence. May seem to indicate.
The culture's neglect. To
recognise the relation of females

to death. Get out of our paper.
Leave our lounge. You phantom
you ghost-girl you cold question

mark. We are not reading. We
cover our eyes. We are throwing
you out with. This newspaper lies.

V. Re-stor(y)ation

I am the mistress of parody
I negotiate the boundary
between inside and out with
miraculous display   You say
I am crazy   you say I am

ill   you don't understand
my idea   I censor the body
to liberate flesh   I erase the
speech to open up breath
What do you know about

over-compliance   defiance
through excess?   What do
you know of perfection?
You sit in the conference
fold upon fold of beige

velvet need   You sit in a
body you don't comprehend
I think you wish you were
me   I have worked my
hypothesis beyond hunger

and truth   I have written
the word you hear in your
dream   It is me turns
your nightmare here in my
hand   it is me who walks

through it is me   You think
I *truncate the onset of
womanhood*   you think I
care about *biology* or
love   I say you think wrong

your *pathology* the prayer
of your own empty pain
your *conclusion* the zen
of your own sad past   That
my *syndrome* has little to do

with your god   that my
sickness is really your own
Why do you stare?   Why do
you prod poke pull at my
parts?   You crazy?   You

ill?   You after the answer
to marital distress?   Maybe
you should eat   Takes away
fear   Maybe you should
swallow the prescribed bitter

pill   But don't come to me
with your instruments of
longing   Don't come to
me with your white gown
cover-up   hides only scars

the smack too many   the
letter goodbye   Don't
make me bite the hand that
feeds   falsity   alibis   I
have no stomach for lies

VI. Her Figure of Speech

Language incarnate   this
urgent text which demands
to be read to the *ostinato*
of pulse   Not the novel

the recording the seascape
on the wall that hangs to
the echo of authorial
demise   this is the story

of imaginative flesh   Eat
the last page no return no
beginning no rereading the
book closed back on its

hinges of irony paradox
metaphor death   Hunger
the punch-line   starvation
the final say   we devour

what we can   curious
bloated   experts in plenty
grown fat on the spectacle
of emaciated need   Study

the form ignore the lived
narrative   develop the
theme the well-rounded
theory   her empty belly

our career   her denial
our ribbon   her obsession
the academic banquet we
invite her to swallow

TREES

They are the complete beings   tall
slim   bending only to a system of
breezes   No fashion here no twigs
snapped to fit the brief idea   no rib
removed no leaf plucked to bare the

brow no bark pared to expose the sin
within   I tread the bush floor
searching for it   the hint the hair-
line crack the breach in the whole
Is there no pornography here?   My

hand is on a leg   a shaft   feeling
fingering the rough reality of another
way   These trees do not war   Their
sex is quiet   comparable to no theory
of mine   No penetration no invasion

of trunk tongue   obscenity gun do not
touch   Please do not feed the trees
They do not hunger   They do not seethe
or writhe   requiring the control of
nylon silk   twisted   root bound foot

spiked heel   Their silence is quite
precise   They know what price has been
exacted of me   They know my loss
Will they love me still?   I am no
great lover   my tap root is unsure my

branches stiff my leaves curled into
themselves   I am steeped in hybridity
confused as to my species   fearful of
love hatred the indifferent sky   If
I stand still   maybe waver a little

If I peel off the layers of polite
conversation   Tuesday   atomic smog
will they know?   If I suck with my
toes uncurl my fingers will they
nod in communion with me?   Is there

room in this crowd for another?
I begin to undress   they appear to say
Yes as they sway   My shoes are
flung far into forest   down
through the tunnel the warren the

memory of female distress   My
breasts fall free my torso expands
hair covers my flesh like a friend   I
feel my roots burgeon back down the
years   I stretch and stand to leave

SCANNING THE TEXT

you are the book   my
careful read   letter
by word   I begin
the stories   faith by
flesh   strength by spine
stamina by secret
desire   no map no
science to guide inside
this   cryptic script
hieroglyphic eyes   I
watch the body for the
plot   design of hope
the sign the mark   held
like a flag against
fright   decode the
cypher   the sub-text of
silence   and scatter
my selves   quiet as
ash   across the unread
pages of your heart

UTTERANCE

Thrown like a symbol into
semantic arrangement I
sign forward quietly vowel
sound by sound   The rules
have fallen in one textual

sigh   I tread through my
papers reading rereading
searching the small print
for something to suck   I
have not read this system

before   the significant
song syntactic display the
urgent lurching linguistic
moan   You are a consonant
aren't you   phonetic event

according to the part of my
mouth you were formed I
sense you standing   mono-
syllabic   tonguing my space
with dialectic desire   I

have not spoken   this
dictionary breast   this
holophrastic heart   beaten
before meaning could enter
me there   You have been

implied   diver for discourse
word between thighs   I
lend you my language for the
length of this line   unfinished
poem and sentence sublime

Eight (Love) Sonnets

I.

When you extend a finger and trace
a trail of comets across the face
of my flesh   I am lit with a hundred
stars. A celestial garden is conjured
inside and tiny buds tap against my
chest   slow to begin with   and shy
as an orchard of Carmelite candles
whose flames are leaves in the mantle
of my breast. Between your arms
I am held in space. The sun warms
my spine and the moon lights my eye
as your burning heart starts to occupy
mine. I feel a locked inner door move
while planets turn knowingly above.

II.

Sometimes my heart is clay-like and
dormant and love alone can travel
the complication of veins that ravel
this body of mine. I can understand
the thread linking forearm to hand
muscles to motion   and the cavel
of bones that sponsor the primeval
design   but the silent life of gland

and marrow   the intricate structure
of memory   nerves   the secret of
life at the uterine/fallopian juncture
the renewal of blood   the shove
of lungs   and the monthly rupture
are known to me only through love.

III.

I open my being to the silver exchange
lovers live by   the currency of salt
steeped in specific fluids   the strange
wines of intimacy   the scarlet gestalt
of a menstrual existence   slipstreams
in armpits   saliva between thighs
a still lake of sweat at a nape. It seems
we trade with our tongues. I recognise
love when I taste your flesh. I name
your heart when I employ my mouth.
I perceive the flavour of your claim
on my senses. And when we have both
transacted any liquid that just might
be love   I open my being to the night.

IV.

After each little death I check
my scars to see I am still alive.
My flesh recalls each wreck
and break of hide   each rive
of pelt   each wounding mark
my body has survived. Above
one eye I trace a sunken arc
of skin   still there   a mauve
remind of where the axe went
in. And at the top of my right
thigh   a symbol   silver rent
of derma   record of my fight
with fire   secret proof that I
return   each tiny time I die.

V.

My body is a laboratory for testing
truth of touch. Dip a litmus finger
in   enter data   but do not linger
in the red-lined hall where questing
types have fallen in the contesting
of my heart. A crimson churinga
hangs inside   cervical harbinger
to cry out loud   at any molesting

thing. Nerves remember and cells
recall (in scientific code) the sting
of flesh entered   and broken. My
methods are modern   I am well-
designed to identify the offending
hand   by the way the fingers lie.

VI.

Be gentle with my arteries   my entire
lymphatic system   my labia   my fat
my soft-veined breasts   and the choir
of tiny hairs along my abdomen that
stands to sing when caressed. Be kind
to my larynx and the base of my neck
my toetips and fingertips   my uterine
part   the invisible ovaries bedecked
with life   the bones of my rib-cage
articulate in pairs   the whites of my
eyes   and my thighs striated with age.
Be patient with my heart as you die
inside me   there are numerous doors
to unclose before it beats beside yours.

VII.

I have little faith in atmospheres
strategies of breathing   I have
lived well enough without love.
My heart has beaten airless here

ozone hole below my left breast
lungs dead empty   diaphragm
flat   respiratory tract jammed
for years. You gave me breath

when we met. You opened my
throat to the passion of oxygen
(symbol O   atomic weight 16)
when your lips made me sigh

with a kiss. That first shock of
air unlocked this body to love.

VIII.

Look closely now. I am coiled like
ivy amongst the villi of your heart.
I am a snake around your psyche.
My reptilian eyes are the only part
of me moving. Look closer now.
I am the ophidian you have seen
in your sleep   the thing you saw
crawl the floor of your dream
when you thought you were alone.
I am a limbless vertebrate. I wind
myself between muscle and bone.
I spiral the bronchi of your mind.
It is my love you feel reeling you
in. I belong to the serpentine few.

The Deep Wait

I am fully entered and then
you are gone.   My waiting works
like scissors or legs   closing
over love with a dreamy flapping
wing.   I am beginning to long.

In the high bright rock   miles
from horizons   I watch my thigh
quiver for hours.   It has brought you
in   carried you out.   It stirs like a
feather.   It hovers the wind.

GOING TO CARRARA

(for Alex Skovron)

Going to Carrara   it is the morning
of lonely perfection.   The sleep
of stone has woken to white
the stone of sleep mere dust in the
eye   the night a dream of rubble.

The sun blinds on a featureless
face   this clever cliff   lighting
the precise idea.   He knows the
rock   the furious faultline vesuvian
god: he breathes once and knows

That is the block.   It is limestone
in a crystalline state   hard as
breast   crumbly as love   capable
of taking a polish.   He fingers the
monument   complete   uncut

straps its map to the small of his back.
Doesn't recall the pathological haul
stumble of theory the basement door.
Sees only the form in the marbly
heart.   Remembers nothing but art.

The sweat of suggestion division of
cells the noise of gestation blood
fast.   Nothing will happen again.
Big blocks like dragons lie dead on
the ground   smaller chips falling

from shoulder and chin   there is but
one way in   the chisel the needle the
faithful pain   the cry of the dying
slave.   The pietà is panting   the child
is out   there is nothing left to save.

This Chiropractic Heart

I live and I live this
chiropractic heart, massage
to muscle, nurture to

nerve, solace to subluxation.
It is my quiet alignment
my beating bone: I know

when it slows and the
drone of drums when they
come. I know the red

arterial confusion, the
aortic thump, ventricular
dread, the coronary

possibility. Blood is just
poetry. I follow it down
the wasted wild, the hollow

hill: I let the fire discern.
Place your hand, feel my rib.
Allow the vermilion flow.

I am all unlocked.
My heart is open.
All my iliacs burn.

FRANKENSTEIN SPEAKS

> *. . . self cannot be united with other*
> *without ceasing to be . . .*
> — *Rosemary Jackson*

In the room of the higher self I
labour. Moon chases sun   this
maniacal pursuit   and desire is
the fix for such radical alchemy.
In my ovarian soul   an idea

dark seed. Who has conceived
such bastardy before? The tumour
of ambition has thrust its root
my smile is secular   I long for
the old absolute. God the Mother

I seek my significance   the air
strains to the tolling of rational
bells. (To examine the causes of
life we must first have recourse
to death   to death.) I undo my

soul   this bold question I house
and mockery clones the pulsating
cry   *I am I am and I am!* And I
have dreamed large   I have
toiled for an age. See his frame

sleepy hulk   cadaver grotesque
at rest in a state of supernatural
suspension. End of November.
A dreary night   each gestation
screams for its delicate conclusion.

Galvanism mesmerism electricity.
I apply the quivering instrument.
Wait for the gasp   the first
searing breath   look my progeny
in the yellowed eye. Is it a boy?

Is he beautiful? The sour truth
leers   he does not even look like
me. I have birthed a stranger-
child   the unsame self   there is
no filial eye to recognise. The bell

in my ear sounds thrice. No infant
yowls but this other arises   eight
foot of offspring   how will he
ever fit back in my head? I feel my
soul tremble   sore cleavage of

self   my desire breathes full and
foul in my face. What now? No
mother can murder his child   fold
him back in the crack he forced
through. An exile in an instant

I trespass the real   bear the
full doom of eternal life. Nature
culture science   the pointed
finger unwavers. Conceptual.
Dread. Monstrosity. Born. An

abortion to spurn kick trample
upon. Who will forgive my
excesses now? I cannot share
the same air   with this daemon
desire   I have unleashed the

unnameable tonight. Where can
I hide? My intent is split like
an amorphous amoeba   huge
with unfill   double-tongued but
no droplet of milk. And listen

he murmurs   my own speechless
woe   inarticulate former self!
My sacred inside it has voice it has
form   this monster is not unique.
I forfeit all innocence (to return

to that realm we must first have
recourse to death). He flees and I
follow   am bound for the same
cold vanishing point   vast terrain.
Denying infinity   the primal cry

sounds   *I was I was and*   I was
torn   asleep   torn   asleep in a
misshapen dream where the mute
goad eloquent and the future defies
time inconsequential   suspended

identity   the everlasting ices
of the North. He lopes with more
than mortal speed   I stumble
behind   dragged by the umbilicus
of lawless desire. What shabby

migration of the popular soul!
I squint   midnight sun   and the
snow snaps back. The mountains
re-echo   I am all around   and
what wretched sound in my ear.

A consummation a consummation.
What man can avoid such a call?
See us traverse the expanse of
Who am I   two fanatical
fragments in pursuit of self. Is

this what I came for is this what
I came for? I deliver my cry of
vengeance ecstatic   he grins
blank satisfaction. This place can
not hold us both   my fiend   yet

what is one   without the other?
This polar region   this region
of polarities   its answer is white
with finality. I see we are joined
I see we are divided. Enemies.

Lovers. Comrades in science.
Let us proceed by negation   the
foreplay of existence   let us
complete this course to full term.
A test to the end   orgasm

profound   I shall not blink in
the face of this other. My desire
hurtles onward. Singularity. Self.
I pursue my own end pursues me.
Hello hello hello   hello   each

echo gives birth to another   an
other. This arctic conundrum. A
room full of mirrors. No god pulls
the play but my self and my self.
A man was created for such sport!

The soulscape opens wide its
chilled arms   destiny freezes and
seals with a glacial kiss. Still we
are flung forth. I cannot live with
without him. I propose the ultimate

marriage. And every thing slows.
I remember the timeless   you
were but an idea   I was one with
the other   a cloud in the mirror.
(The ice smiles a hairline crack.)

I steel-willed you   trance-formed
you   I wagged my genius at God.
And you rocked in the harbour
of my amniotic intellect like a boat
on a sea of sin. (Smile becomes

grimace becomes chasm.) *You were*
my poem perpetual   my ever
after   (becomes laugh   becomes
breach   cracked world). Now it is
over. It is done. Who hears the

death bell toll in his ear? It is
the wedding march! I lurch to my
self   that ultimate embrace (the
iceberg divides) and hug the serial
ream of my being. It is unity

I have so ardently sought. Come
foul other   we have seduced our
self (we drift apart). To examine
our life we must first have recourse
to   (everything merges to white

NOTES

FRIDA KAHLO: AN EXHIBITION

Magdalena Carmen Frida Kahlo Y Calderón was born in Mexico City, in 1907.

On September 17, 1925, the bus Frida was riding was hit by a trolley car. The impact of the collision impaled her body on an iron rod. In the accident, Frida's clothes were torn off and her body covered with gold dust which a fellow traveller had spilled. Although she never painted the actual event, her self-portraits are haunted by the central theme of the injuries she incurred at the time.

After a lifetime of operations and narcotics, Frida died in 1954. She is best known for her collection of self-portraits where she exhibits herself as icon, still-life, and mesmeric *retablo*.

Frida was married to renowned Mexican muralist Diego Rivera. She had no children.

BLACK IRIS III

Georgia O'Keeffe (1887–1986) was a leading American artist whose long life produced a large and varied collection of works. Most of her paintings look to nature for their impetus – the South-West American landscape, flowers, skulls, the deserts of New Mexico – and are dominated by abstractions in watercolour.

Black Iris III (1926) is a close and contemplative floral study in oils.

THE SALEM PAPERS, 1692

The Salem witchcraft delusion, like any significant historical event, did not take place in a cultural vacuum. Certain factors converged in the year of 1692 to create an environment in which the accusation of almost two hundred people from a total of twenty-two towns in New England seemed warranted. By the time of its conclusion nineteen of the accused had been hanged, one had been pressed to death, and eight had died in prison. Many others had suffered serious losses, including land, chattels, money spent on prison fees and, perhaps most importantly, the loss of a reputation untainted by the cry of witch.

A collection of court transcripts survives, in which the examinations of many of the accused are recorded. These documents are the inspiration behind "The Salem Papers, 1692".

SUSANNA AND THE ELDERS

"The History of Susanna" does not appear in the Bible, but is one of the fourteen stories comprising The Apocrypha. Set apart "because it is not in the Hebrew", it represents a subversive story in terms of both content, and language.

The story describes Susanna's beauty, and the lust two elderly judges had for her. Seeing her in her husband's garden every day, the two men devised a rape strategy based on blackmail. The pair planned to confront Susanna when she was alone and demand she "lie" with them: if she refused, they would tell the authorities they had seen her with a young man, and Susanna would face punishment of death.

Susanna refused to consent, and the elders followed through with their threat. Their story was believed (as hers was not), and Susanna was sentenced to die. Her life was saved by another man, Daniel, who interviewed the elders separately, thus exposing discrepancies in their tales.

The Body in Time

Diane Fahey

About Diane Fahey

Diane Fahey grew up in Melbourne, lived in Britain in the early 80s, and moved to Adelaide in 1986. She has spent the last few years living in NSW, Britain, and – presently – Victoria.

Her poetry features distinctively Australian, and European, settings and preoccupations. Dominant concerns are Greek myth, feminism, art, landscape, and, increasingly, ecological themes.

She has won various awards including the Mattara Poetry Prize and the Wesley Michel Wright Poetry Prize, and has received three Writer's Fellowships from the Literature Board of the Australia Council, and Writer's Grants from the South Australian, and Victorian governments.

In 1993 she was a Fellow at Hawthornden International Writers' Retreat, Scotland.

ALSO BY DIANE FAHEY

Voices from the Honeycomb (Jacaranda)
Metamorphoses (Dangaroo)
Turning the Hourglass (Dangaroo)
Mayflies in Amber (A&R/HarperCollins)

Acknowledgements

This work was assisted by a writer's fellowship from the Literature Board of the Australia Council, the Federal Government's arts funding and advisory body, and by the South Australian Government through the Department of the Arts and Cultural Development.

My grateful thanks are also due to the Eleanor Dark Foundation for a residential fellowship at "Varuna — a Writers' Centre" in 1991, with particular thanks to Michael and Jill Dark; and to Mrs Drue Heinz for the awarding of a residential fellowship at Hawthornden Castle International Writers' Retreat in 1993. Parts of this work were written, and other parts revised, during these residencies. "Venice Notebook" was written during a residency in Venice in 1987, funded by the Literature Board of the Australia Council.

Poems in this collection were published in: the *Age*, *Australian Women's Book Review*, the *Bulletin*, the *Canberra Times*, the *Courier-Mail*, *Hope and Fear: An Anthology of SA Women's Writing*, *Imago*, *Into the Nineties: Post-Colonial Women's Writing*, *Island*, *Meanjin*, *Northern Perspective*, *Ormond Papers 1994*, *Overland*, *Second Degree Tampering: Writing by Women*, *Southerly*, *Southern Review*, the *Sydney Morning Herald*, *Tarantella*, *Voices* (Australia); *Ariel* (Canada); *New Poetry Review*, *Resurgence*, *Verse* (England); *Poetry Ireland*; *New Welsh Review*, *Planet*, *Poetry Wales*; *Antipodes* (USA).

Some poems were broadcast by the ABC, and 5UV (Adelaide).

The Body in Time

CONTENTS

4. In Memory

5. SITES

The Body in Time

MOVIEGOER

It was
the Kinema at Albert Park for matinées on Saturday:
Ma and Pa Kettle, *The Three Stooges*, *Brigadoon*.
Chips afterwards, a walk through empty streets,
the park with bowlers. Sometimes, boys circling
closer on bikes, skidding to expose themselves. . .
We ran, us girls, clutching the last of our chips;
once, after a Blue Heaven milkshake, I was sick.

Twice a week we frequented, my family and I,
the Empire – alias the Bughouse. In dusk light
we ambled down the hill, through lanes
dotted with bins to Coventry Street. It was
June and Van, Doris and Rock, Paul and Joanne. . .
In over-large dress, neat cardigan, white socks,
I hid in the Ladies' as Rita Hayworth danced
the Dance of the Seven Veils – one mortal sin
avoided; seven of them. It seemed an eternity,
waiting in there on crimson concrete, among
clammy smells, while the back-row girls came
to relieve themselves, fix make-up, gossip
about boys. They had beehive hairdos, waists
cinched by huge elastic bands, mascara-black.
Ken the usher's torch, searchlight of decency,
was no match for them, going the whole way,
somehow, in bucket seats, slipping and sliding
in the Brylcreem darkness. . .

I never saw that body
pretend to bare itself on screen, only the beheading
after: so many meanings given to the nakedness
of woman. But what did I know of that, then?
At interval, orange or sarsaparilla in fluted glasses –

121

elongated chalices waiting in rows on the counter.
Later, we made for home, past back gates
and broken fences, up the hill to where we'd sleep,
dream gaudily fearful dreams, under
the moonlit shadow of the Town Hall clocktower.

Thirteen

I was practising being a saint.
My brown lace-ups were clamped
to the dusty floor, and I was in them.
The mirror, an oval drop
of flat untrembling water, showed
a pale girl inside a yellow raincoat.
I hated it. 'This one,' I said.
My mother passed the silky beige one,
the dearer one, back to the woman,
and softly they agreed: 'Too young
to know its value.'

               'Some of us even
wear yellow raincoats to school!'
The nun stood on a bench –
wasp-waisted, her cheeks covered
with tributaries of red lightning.
Her eyes glittered as two hundred girls
marched with military precision
round the playground. In tune
with a deeper instinct, I dragged
my feet into the asphalt,
waiting to be detected, punished. . .
She was the one who ground me down
the way she ground her yellow teeth,
and almost triumphed –
until the day when, kindled with rage,
she struck me across the arm:
'Get out, then!' And I had won,
my eyes drops of flat untrembling water,
giving her back her hatred,
polishing it with the fresh shine of youth.

Some of Us Even/If Only/Don't

When I was seven, a nun said,
   'Some of us even get our picture in the paper
      wearing shorts.'
When I was nine, a nun said,
   'Some of us even whistle while we are walking
      home from school.'
When I was twelve, one said,
   'Don't tie your hair back, you look like
      a washerwoman'
and
   'If only your name were Mary Diane, not
      Diane Mary'
and – when I changed the calendar from March
      to April –
   'Pin the page back. And don't touch what you
      don't understand.'
(It was April.)

Our names, our voices, our clothes, our hair,
our knowledge that time, left to itself, goes
      forwards. . .
Moved by fear, spite, lack, you tried to change
      these things.

Memory sweeps the crypt, dusts small moments
      of dying.
Her hair is hidden, she wears black, is voiceless,
      nameless;
the watch tied to her wrist runs backwards.

Ten

Too young to notice the transfiguration
of my flowered blue pyjamas;
too young to understand, had I been told.

Something explosive, unpredictable, inside,
that's how it felt – a weight at your centre
that stopped you from running free,
forgetting you were thinking.

An end to childhood's botched dream. . .

But time makes us used to so many things –
however unritualised
new meanings settle into our lives.

We are placed in the middle of a labyrinth;
slowly, we learn how to give birth,
make what is infolded, manifest:

heart and womb;
        moon and sea;
                in command/at the mercy.

NINE/ELEVEN/FIVE

'Good things come in little parcels.'
He said it twice, my uncle,
with a mischievous smile.

It was a manicure set.
It was my birthday. I was nine.

At eleven, in the spare room,
I'd wake early, listen to every sound –
polishing of boots, bathroom taps –
as he made ready for work.

Always neat and well-organised,
a meticulous man.

I kept petticoat and all on
under my nightie. My aunt said,
when she found out, 'That's dirty.'

Year after year
I went there for holidays.
Why don't I remember?

At five, in the tool shed,
I told him to put me down. 'Why,'
he said, 'why, what's wrong?'
in a soft voice.

And I walked up the yard,
through the sunlight,
with an immense dignity,

knowing I would not speak of it,
knowing.

CHURCH-GOING

Accosted, near childhood's end.
'Want a piss?' he said, 'Want a piss?'

Dorcas Street. Blank winter light.
Already late for mass, I ran.

His eyes were quick and dark as
an animal's: between mouse and rat. . .

As I grew up, I saw him around
the place – alone, with women.

The one with balding red hair,
skin tight on flaccid body,

the one who'd pestered me on the tram –
I saw him often at church,

would stare through his toadish look:
pink whisky-man in caramel suit.

Then Father Dunphy with his retreats:
black *metanoia* as he roared up details

of botched abortions, foetuses wrapped
in newspaper, crying from dustbins.

Agape, Eros – they were abortions, too.

Wanting to know what I did not know,
frightened of it all, each night

I struggled in with spiky heels,
suspended nylons, all awkwardly new.

At its ripening, the body turns oceanic,
hungers to take and give life.

Marble stations of the cross. Peccadillos
whispered from a carved wood box.

*I have come that you may have life,
and have it more abundantly.*

PEBBLES

Hamstrung by pain and silliness
we hobbled the martyr trail to mass:
'Claudia, just this sharp one –
under my little toe – it's killing me!'

If suffering accepted brought down
grace, what price this chosen
agony of stones?

(No one told of the suffering
that squats for years on your shoulders,
destroys all memory of grace.)

But mostly, in those days,
it was lolling on beds at Claudia's place.
We read film star magazines, talked
of her older sisters – all stylish
and grown up and complicated.

At meals there were arguments
and grapes, the smell of olive oil.

In that home, I lived out
suppressed desires: taught myself
my first and only piano piece;
read, with a sense of hollow sin,
A *Certain Smile:* such a thin book,
her face so pale on the cover. . .

No answers there! Oh, but to know
what Giovanna and Renata knew!
(About love bites, say, which almost

made me faint – lust-bruises!
beast-marks on the neck!)

But they thought *Carousel*
was crap – that really hurt. . .

Things were almost as
they should have been, then,
        I now see:
intimations of an ease in life,
truth mixed with warmth,
a sensual honesty.

FIFTEEN

Black statues moving around the room,
     the Brothers were up against it:
screening the practice school dance for
     groin-crushers.

My partner was Joe. What a letdown I was –
     as naive as the day is long
while resisting unto death that conscious thrust,
     insistent stare.

I never dreamt of screaming, or walking out,
     did not presume to feel anger,
the room guttering inside my head as I swallowed
     humiliation.

I even suffered because I bored him – nerveless,
     determined Joe,
good-looking, with curly yellow hair. In the breaks,
     he made off

with his pal, both close, tight-lipped, somehow
     in it together.
(What, for god's sake, were they whispering about
     out there?)

On the night of the real dance, he dumped me.
     Who could blame him?
Sue stole the evening, blancmange breasts aquiver
     above crimson.

Angry as blackbirds, the Brothers confabulated
     in corners,
mindful, no doubt, of the moral theology of it all –

how a strapless dress is, *ipso facto*, an occasion
      of sin: fantasies
of gowns falling to the floor, bare bodies, the whole
      damned thing.

And, to add insult to injury, there was Claudia's
      cleavage,
olive-toned and wonderful, rising from cobalt silk. . .

Generous as flesh, or mean as sin, there is no
      gainsaying sex –
spied on, it becomes invisible, can hide in the cells
      for a lifetime.

After the dance, I set out to walk from Northcote
      to South Melbourne –
that's how I felt. 'Oh, Joe will bring me back,'
      I'd said,

waving a taxi fare away at the kitchen table.
      It was Philip
who brought me home. Nice-looking and quiet,
      he knew me

from a distance. 'Come out on Sunday,' he said,
      'for a drive.'
I don't know how many times I got up to put fresh
      lipstick on.

He never came. That was my first real date.
      The one with Joe
doesn't count, arranged, as it was, between
      the schools –

lists of partners drawn up by the Sisters and
      the Brothers.

Eighteen

At the University of Melbourne

. . . acute loneliness seems to be the most painful kind of anxiety
that a human being can suffer. Patients often tell us that the pain
is a physical gnawing in their chests, or feels like the cutting of a
razor in their heart region. . .

Rollo May, *Love and Will*

Tiny boys in beige suits with shoulder pads;
girls compact as almonds in pink tulle.

On the plateau above the car park
an Italian-Indonesian wedding
being photographed against sandstone.

At the reception will there be
pasta with peanut sauce,
satay neapolitan?

The couple look into each other's eyes,
not needing youth,
in the throes of something else. . .

    Thirty years ago I walked under
    these plane trees with a sword
    stuck through my heart –

    not knowing, quite, what to do with it,
    not taking myself too seriously,
    almost, in the end, seeing the funny side. . .

    Now, old scars invisible,
    the only problem is
    these seeds in heart-flesh
    that cannot flower.

As if on a great sundial
that edge of shadow creeps
over well-shod feet;

over romantic love,
two intersecting tribes,
the wedding industry.

> In sickness and in health
> I have lived the loneliness.

> Is this the learning life asks of me:
> to turn sword into ploughshare,
> forge long furrows of words?

> The years are a sundial;
> I stand on an edge of shadow –
> moving which way?

There is sunlight, still,
on the faces of the wedding guests,
overdressed infants with stunned eyes
now carried in arms:

they do not know they are
a rehearsal for a poem –
another attempt to come to terms.

The colour of the stone
is mixed honey and clay,
untouched by the decades
I am glad are over

as life throws up scenarios
of burgeoning and risk and bravura,

and offers moments
when that which has been rent asunder
comes together.

WHENEVER IT WAS

Our Lady's Primary School, South Melbourne

There was Miss Quinn with her pearls and exactitude
and fuzzy wuzzy jumpers

and nuns who were angels or hyenas

and, in my lemon taffeta dress with sparkly stuff,
me, at the school ball, wetting myself

and being told, in front of the whole school,
'You look like you've got a balloon under your dress,'
when we were practising the balloon dance
out in the yard, and I wished the asphalt
would open black jaws and gobble me

and there was the baiting of Sister Gerardus –
blushingly shy in middle age – as she sat,
crippled with tears, in her sewing class,
and they worked away till her soul lay bare
as an unpicked seam

and there were the check tablecloths I edged
in rickrack and patterned with cross stitch,
and the sampler – warm yellow, the colour
of sanity – I threaded with silken runes:
my first poem;

there was Sister Dorothea, as sweet
as spring light – too gentle to survive elsewhere,
but strong here, in the way freesias
or lilies of the valley are strong

and others like tanks or zeppelins draped in black
warning a captive chapelful against bad thoughts,
before Benediction with Father So-And-So –
the meat in a chasuble sandwich –

and weirdly sensual spiritual incense
swung towards us, a fading cloud
seeking each of us out with amorphous fingers;

there were the doctors who – with careful,
masonic nods – laughed at the holy medal
tied to my belt with twisted hat elastic
when we were lined up to be inoculated

and the Hansen girls from an abusing home
with their shame at rusty, holed underwear
when other doctors came and we had to undress
and have stethoscopes, and nurses who
looked down our pants (a search for hermaphrodites?)

and there were the convent girls with chilblains
and bold ways and crushes on nuns. They got the strap
most often, called the rest of us, 'yews girls',
and said we were bold, and would get into trouble

and there was listening to Bing Crosby read
'The Little Prince' ('Oh, swallow, swallow,
little swallow'), and trying not to cry

and learning by rote 'The Tarantella', and the one
about Mar-ga-ret, and 'The Wreck of the Hesperus'
to be futilely tested each day after lunch;

there was falling on cobbles as I ran home
and having Bates' Salve, hot, that my father swore by,
with its funny brown smell, melt into my knee

and there were swap cards (my favorite,
'The Blue Boy') – their incandescence
a promise of other worlds – friendships
were gained and lost in fights over them

and sticking up for Barbara, who was fat,
and always, myself, feeling outside things
even when I was in them

and there was the strapping from Sister Gilberta
when she lost control, and I could not
stop crying so that, in panic, she sent me home
and I started walking with blotched face
and unearthly pauses between sobs

though there was the day I broke
the diamond blue glass round Our Lady's candle,
and she took it like a saint –
her one moment of restraint is at my door

and there was the liquid scrambled egg
at my First Communion lunch after kneeling
in church trying to feel religious
and singing oozy, bleating hymns
then trying to unstick jesus-in-the-host
from the dry roof of my mouth:
if it was a sacrilege at least no one knew –
except You-Know-Who. . .

At the height of a hot summer, I see us
kneeling on the floor, bone against wood –
grades five and six, in our double room –
chanting decade after decade of the rosary,

watching the pictures some of us had painted
turned round and round in a wooden box.
I always waited for mine, 'The Crucifixion',
which I thought the best.

In the first three grades when there were
boys, I remember the one called Mickey Mouse
they let be cheeky, and myself
standing apart and looking, and not being
one of the favorites of Sister Angela
with her golden tooth and golden smile.

I remember the red chalk apple on the board –
A for APPLE, and my mother's squashy
tomato sandwiches, and being so unhappy
I went to St Peter and Paul's, and did
a jam jar covered in wet newspaper pulp,
but returned to Our Lady's because
I was still unhappy: I did this twice.
I never painted the jam jar.

Towards the end, thinking I was
inventing something, I drew strange
vectors and tangents on a page
in my geometry book, and Sister Dorothea,
a patient woman, lost patience,
but I got a scholarship anyway –
one of three who would go on. . .
Joan and Gillian were the others.

Childhood ended with hallucinations
of a great black dog with lantern eyes
roaring up from hell through the shadows
beside my white wardrobe.

Between the paralysis
and the hand's agonising crawl
to reach wet forehead and invoke,
with famous words, the homosexual
trinity, I lived an eternity.

Volition wrested from nightmare.

In one of my books an old philosopher
in prison staved off blindness
by bathing his eyes each day
with drops of water. So he read on,
could go on being who he was.
Could go on and on. . .

In Love and Hate

HEATH WALK

Late summer now,
we are used to each other,
walk with linked arms
towards the pool. I sit
watching green light,
green darkness, flow
together over water.
You go to swim under
the trees, but stay
on the concrete ledge
fathoming the water's
chill, the shock of it
against your body,
no longer young.
You stroll towards me,
dress, as day turns
to evening. The pond
is given back to ducks
and fishing lines,
the last swimmer risen
through its gleam.
Air is keen on our skin,
we pass between
trees bearing night's
coolness, with, as yet,
no hint of drying.

RECONCILIATION

Alone on the roof:
the sun burns under my skin;

lining eyelids, barely closed,
the sky's canopy blazes. . .

Tonight, if we are reconciled,
I will lie, as now,

holding my own heat, yours,
feel the thirst rise

from throat cavern, root of tongue:
we will lend our moistures

to each other, we will plummet
sensing the sky's height

and, beneath, tingling dark depths.
Around us, water that bathes and heals,

salt that promises fresh thirst.

SLEEP

What bonded us
seemed too deep to name.

What could separate us?

I think it will be
the usual commonplaces –

misunderstanding,
fear, false hope –

expressing, in our case,
incompatible life-damage.

Just now, you sleep,
your black lashes unmoving

beneath eyelids
changing shape in dream.

The candle by the bed
lights our faces

which consume, throw back,
the room's darkness.

In the Half-light

A woman kneels before him
washing his feet

slowly, sensuously.
She wishes her long hair

were long enough to dry them.
In the unbreathing silence, he says,

'I don't want you to do this' –
lying as usual.

She continues
until it is over.

She will remember this as
the one moment of fulfilment,

the only moment
when she was free of fear.

WEEKEND AWAY

A landlady with sour lips, mistrustful eyes. . .
I lay beside you in pink nylon sheets
and rubbed you warm in your feverish chill,
curving against your side, asking nothing.
That closeness could not dispel your fever,
or the barriers between us.

                     Earlier that day
we'd clambered on muddy stones to reach
the poet's house, tucked in beneath a cliff,
the sea exploding into air like alcohol into
the veins. No trace here of the man who would
drink himself to death. Next morning,
the journey home, choking with separateness,
mile after violent mile, covering no new
ground, moving back into old darknesses.

Smoking in Bed

Months of illness
from which you could not recover,

bled dry by the succubus, the handsome stranger
who came to your bed each night

keeping you awake to keep him company
as he smoked in the half-darkness,

drunk, listening to the Eagles, Bob Dylan,
whoever. . . To hear any of those songs again

is to lie there coughing
week after week until

finally you told him straight
to put out his cigarette,

knowing you might die before
he took the hint.

His look of disbelief
is what you have to thank

for the long slow roll of amusement
that washed over you –

amusement it would not, at the time,
have been wise to express –

leading you, despite your stupidity,
by the nose out of all that misery.

SEVERANCE

Now I understand your fear, distrust,
were even greater than mine –

with some reason, perhaps,
as you may well have guessed

that I could write poems like this,
that I would come to see through you

like a broken pane of glass.
You gave me the worst hours and days

of my life, when I lay marvelling
that pain does not kill us outright.

Now you have no claim on me,
rarely touch memory.

POETRY READING

You asked me
why I had chosen to read
the poem of the girl buried at Pompeii,
and, really, I had no idea,
then,

my dear lava, my white-hot ash,

and you were so concerned for me –
When I think about it,
really, I'm quite touched,

my cold lava, my snowstorm of ash.

What You Know

Your lover/enemy
will never absolve you for leaving
while you had something left to give.

You know irrevocably
that you will never again lie powerless
to suit the convenience of another.

You know you will not be remembered
for any solace you offered,
or for your generosity.

Since joy is freedom,
there was no real joy.

It's time to kill all this,
to somehow leave.

TIME'S LIGHT, TIME'S DARKNESS

Love is not so blind
as to regret

its monumental blindness,
the shadow side

of what it touched
and knew;

in a half-lit room,
white spaces in the memory

contracting
inside time's darkness.

The Middle of Life

PRIMAL SCENE

The summons comes at a late hour – so inconvenient:
she's propped against pillows, glass of port to hand,
reading *The Case of the Disappearing Doppelgänger*. . .

A night journey. Soon after eight, she trudges up
        the drive,
refuses tea, strides to the summerhouse. Suddenly,
she's staring down at a vacant space, shaped like
        a body.

No proof of crime yet, but where has this life
        disappeared to?
By nine, they've assembled – the whole jittery cast:
over dark crescent moons, stunned eyes avoid each
        other.

She paces the room, tests each angle and point of view:
that tired woman on the sofa, her hair blurred by
        sunlight –
where's she in all this? And, near the door, looking
        forlorn,

the girl with bitten nails. By the aspidistra, duster in
        hand,
the spruce maid. (That costume's clearly a façade.)
She herself is in drag on this occasion – crossed
        boundaries

can disconcert, help cut to the truth; besides, the best
thinking's done in a collar and tie – or so they say. . .
Using her watch as an *aide-mémoire*, she starts
        the questions.

Later, strolling the garden – how all those faces seem
like flowers! – she notes a sundial fringed by daisies:
a dance of asterisks shadows that unequivocal triangle.

Life as a Freudian detective story! – what can't or won't
they remember about what did her in, made her just
fade away? Who holds the key? Will any clues be found?

At one point a child had run across the room – plump,
with dark curls, an unfrilled dress. Whom did she
            run to,
look away from? Quick, write it down before it's lost!

The time has come for her to stand in that void
outlined on the floor, stare everyone hard in the eye,
say something eccentric, and leave. . . Return to Start:

it's a real board game getting back to where she came
            from,
but, at the other end, the book lies open on the table,
the port glints. They're assembled in the summer-
            house.

It's Sunday, the air outside balmy – a trampoline
            for bees.
Inside, humidity. They watch me circle then enter
that mummy-shaped form. This is the optimum
            moment:

if there's to be a revelation it must come *now*. . . I turn,
meet each pair of eyes – all blue-green, like my own.
After a tortuous silence, an unexpected voice begins
            to speak.

WIND

Drag on shoulders and back as you heave this huge
     muscle
coming apart in your hands, spilling away from you,
rush it out among leaves in flux, colliding whispers.

One hoist clumps it over the tightrope: a humped
     shape
flapping absurdist wings. Next, the pull into
     smoothness
as tears roll down arm-veins, fuse skin and wool.

Damp gathers in vortex of navel, the belly moulded,
like breasts and limbs, by an erotic shroud.
You unclasp it to a straight fall, remove the template,

but again and again the wind rehearses those shapes,
invents variations, or erases the body's planes
to conjure ghosts behind curtains, unhuman masks.

Your hair a cubist halo, clothes harlequined by water,
you peg the sheet that knows your impress so well,
has held the sweat of your dreams. It releases into,

now a wildness, now a sedate swaying, forked by
sleep-creases. . . Half-sighs, an austere rustling:
this impersonal fabric has its voices, too.

They tell you to live with your hands on the world,
to wring and uncoil its bundled knots. Your body
     itself
is a subtle knot silhouetted by pure air, its heat

transfiguring cool envelopes you enter, white planes
blankly receiving imprint, a few trace elements,
till whisked away to be drowned then resurrected:

a sail for the winds of heaven to rest against,
curved as cheek or hollow of palm; resisting
and surrendering; teased to life by the merest touch.

DESPAIR

Cover the left side of your face, and see it:
an unwilled bitterness in flesh and feature.
Call it an active lack of expectation –
it replaces fear as your ruling passion,
will be lived with equal single-mindedness:
the killing logic that's your version of piety.

There's defencelessness in it, too –
as of an unquilled porcupine huddling
in your lap: a once bristly reality
become this shapeless, alive, no-being,
utterly at odds with its future.

What to do? Rearrange that face for a start.
Easy: the body is only time-lapse plasticine,
isn't it? Remove all sign of what blocks out
the sorrows of friends, meets the new
with boredom, is in a continental drift
away from wherever now is.

And there's no short-circuiting despair
with cheer or compromise; it will not be
got to the bottom of, or written out in poems.

This has been sent to you, has arisen from
what you are: a ticking bomb to be defused,
a Trojan horse to outwit. Walk round it slowly.
Deal with it or be diminished, become a self
shivering in your own helpless hands
that can make no offering, will damage all gifts.

In The House

Fingers stumble against plates;
a duster flicks ornaments
from their humdrum lives
to splinter on ash-stained hearth;
pot plants noticed too often, die.

Her hand clamps an island
of steak near where she hacks it
as if the flesh of an enemy
newly killed, beyond thought already.

In the end, forks in the drawer
attack her, egg stains return
to scrubbed pans, a whirring bowl
seams a spiral of blood
into creamy blandness.

This is the nemesis sent to one
who does nothing with ease –
the reward for services
rendered in love's absence.

Though it clamours still
for food, the body cries, *All this
is so beside the point!* –

but how can she hear it,
bent to the vacuum's whine
exacting its pound of dust
from shagpile; then that silence

ringing in her ears as
creeper curls through sill
and she imagines the whole house
held in the garden's forced embrace. . .

Her eyes shift to smudges that
censor her face superimposed on
glass figures by a lake;
a moonlit sea-storm; sunflowers

bursting from the frame of
their petals, from molten centres,
each tip a wanton flame
draining the air she breathes.

Rooms

Could one surprise a room,
fling open a door to discover
some unknown mood of silence,
or, in the air, a busyness
one could not quite read –

memories stored in brick flesh
seeping back into space
to be sparked by sunlight
into a sky of milling planets?

Cells shed from tired skin
settle in lesions, joins,
enter wood's susceptibility,

so that body and mind, both,
leave their trace, in a chemistry
that brings tremulous pain
and the brute years, to a stillness.

Even when we breathe elsewhere,
the work is being done,
our elements sift into solidity,
are resurrected as masonry
shifts and white clouds rise
and you cannot see for looking:

the atmosphere of a room
re-entering your skin, your blood –

life recognising itself amidst
dissolution; as foundations stir;
when diamond-blades of light
pierce through and through
what one thought void, done with.

FLOWERS

You are always not noticing them,
and buy them as if they might save you from this,
drawn into lit scented space
by a bunch you think you can get along with –
of marigolds, say –
not too glorious or exotic;
still youthful; just a little thickset.

Green sticks inside glass; orange discs.
You walk away, though what you want
is to be let into their long moment;
more secretly still, you want them
to heal and sustain you. Perhaps they do. . .
But there they go, drooping and dying again
before you've stopped to contemplate,
given them time to reach you.

Now you come into your own – it's too late,
you've missed the best of things, so you hang on,
letting them scatter in pieces, turn to slime.
Hands on hollow stems and muck,
you plunge them into plastic
with fastidious tired guilt;
for days the vase soaks on the sink.

Yes: you'd rather analyse yourself,
labour at poems like this, than consider
a flower. Here is a marigold. . .
Ordinary and luminous; earth-bound,
though Mary the Virgin's gold.
Once sold by the barrel, showered in
broths and stews: to fend off pestilence,
'strengthen and comfort the hart'.
For bee stings, apply fresh petals directly.

ACCIDENT

It could happen like this.
You turn the corner of another
night, wake foot to the floor
as the car around you
slides down a mountain.

Today, a journey to be made. . .
You sit stunned in early light
then clutch the keys, persuaded
the dream relives past crashes –
you've had a string of them.

The odds are longer, now,
you think; in fact, they're shorter.

Out from the city, headed for
shifting white distance. . .
As if you were someone else
you pass through exhaustion,
fear, throat-holds of panic.

Near dusk, it's hunger and
loneliness that propel you,
are the fuel you burn. Then
the mountains weaving you
into their folds, the sudden turn

towards glass and chrome
stopped on asphalt. . . A whirr
of reflexes as despair bursts
inside you. Foot to the floor,
an endless skid on gravel.

The car has become a body
aching with miles, a mind
fraught with intentions.

Once more, a lesson; mercifully,
no injury to persons, only
brute metal: the mudguard is
turned back like a skin flap
from a wound – fine carving.

You pray for eyes
that will see levelly.

IN THE MIDDLE OF LIFE

Breasts silken as at twenty:
the body flirts with time,

fulfilled in its survival of
absence, unanswered need.

Man's prime but woman's fall?
I can abjure that if I choose,

pluck real images of self,
undream the poisoned dream.

In the void that follows grief,
in the trammels of desire,

I plant seeds deep in a desert.

Wordlessness claims me
as, once, I claimed words.

STATEMENT

Years spent with the elegance, the mess,
of words,
practising honesty like a vocation,
tending and attending.

Dreams that riddle day or night
tell a different story:
of the life not lived,
the gulf, the knot, inside the body.

Intimacy: the fear behind decorum;
loneliness wastes you like a disease. . .
You wake breathless,
relearn the humble need for air

while images hold you in their closed fists.
You embrace powerlessness,
sit listening at a distance,
carving sounds on a page.

Untitled

The childlessness that held me
ransom for years, weighting
my flesh, breathing my breath,

has gone, leaving me, as before,
at pains to be responsible for this
one life, try to get it right.

Earlier, I gave birth to my own spirit,
stubbornness the midwife, as I
laboured to be free of so much death.

Now I forge a middle course between
indifference and too much caring,
inhabit this almost accustomed

separateness leavened by friendship
and poetry, mark the constant blue
against green of sky and eucalypt;

rosemary flower and leaf;
the sea's sapphire map
broken by continents of reef.

To an Unknown Lover

Some Definitions

1. Fathom
OE *fæthm:* the outstretched arms

to embrace the depths of
to enfold as with the buoyancy of water

to sound, to penetrate
to touch with the eyes

to know

2. Fixed Star
fixed star: *any of the stars which apparently always*
retain the same position with respect to one another

a stable relativity
a constancy as one shapes one's own orbit

to the distant eye, a clear shining
close up, a molten globe, a fieriness

a true star
a respect for equidistance
     apparently always

3. *Illusion*
L. *illudere*: to sport with; *illusio*: deceit

the mirror offers an illusion of truth

to love the known
is to piece fragments
of a mirror together

so as to conjure the whole.

to love the unknown
is to make space for
the not-yet-born;

to open a door in the night
to the adversary.

the mirror offers the truth of illusion

4. *Gold*
. . . that which resists rust

gold grains in an hourglass
run their course,

lasting beyond death,
or till a word or thought

seeds the end –
that shimmering stream

stopped, the hand
which tries to restore it

breaks the vessel –
splinters of glass

and heart dust,
a jagged gleaming

5. *Still*
   verb – to quiet (wind, waves, commotion, tumult,
      passion, pain etc.)
   adj. – subdued or low in sound; hushed; 'in the stille
      night'
   noun – a distilling apparatus, consisting of a vessel
      in which the substance is heated and vaporized

what fusions of being
will brew from this heat

what alchemies of silence
be born from this

entering into,
this setting free

THE MARRIAGE OF FIGARO

If only real life were so vivid, however confusing:
from far-off, lots of dazzle and noise and speed. . .
Closer in, mouths laugh, shout, kiss – butterfly shapes
collide with passions aflutter, or part with mirrored
doubleness. Constantly, new things are about to happen,
reversals wait in the wings, except when – closer still –
spotlit interludes of pure feeling set forth dilemma,
infolded outcome, like a tarot card.
                                        At the finale,
threads of love and illusion weave a mandala of sound,
with everyone chastened, heartened, eager to go on.
But such hard work! It must be the music that keeps
them cheerful: even *Where are the Happy Times?*
buoyed my spirit for weeks, an echo deep in the mind.
Then, too, they have the consolation of dignity:
the Count gets, not a custard pie, but the Countess,
Figaro's doubts are healed by Susannah's faith,
with Cherubino saved from polymorphous perversity. . .
Reborn unions litter the stage like happy endings:
Eros will have his day now Thanatos the trickster's
been sent packing – until tomorrow's matinée.

THE HANDLESS MAIDEN

One opened, cradling itself:
a bowl of dyadic pink offered
mainland with promontories,
a chaos of rivulets.

There were shallow sharp grooves
as if scratched by nib or quill;
others, etched with deeper intent –
runes, not-to-be-translated.

Behind knuckles, needlework threads:
cobalt-purple as the tracery
on thumbs. At the wrist,
lightning strike of lavender
and almost-aquamarine.

The other stretched out flat
on her lap: five moons about to set
or rising; brown rain staining
earth-flesh. As it turned, light on
ruched silk, river-ripples.

They met, began to
reshape each other, learn
each other, dance. . .

> What to do but go on imagining
> these hands till she could
> grasp on to life and not let go
> before life failed her,
>
> while the poem cupped by
> the fingers' cage sings to soothe
> Death, allay its worst fears,
> coax it into a painless
> light sleep.

ASSEMBLAGE

I wake, re-position my head
carefully back on my shoulders,
revolve the bolt.

Dents in the teapot on my breakfast tray
evoke the dimples, oily
with light, I'll dive into

at the pool – a liquid bowling green
draining through shark gills.
I wear a twenties costume –

black wool, knee to neck –
but anyone can see my skin's
rough patchwork; that my joints

have metal accessories.
I am what I appear to be –
a walking industrial accident.

Though large of stature
I'm less endowed than the life-guard
smirking up from his sleek strut.

Thirsty for reassurance, I lope to
the spa – the circle widens with
distant looks, its temperature rises.

'O! that this too too solid. . .'
But no! Resolute fingers clamp
bubbling thighs, I check my toes.

Sans suit, a businessman rises up –
his body hair that of a new-born ape,
cramped jowls close-shaven.

Back in the change room, I fiddle
with scar cremes, anti-rust spray,
busy as a drag queen.

A half-fogged mirror shows
two eyes, almost level, almost
equally blue, in this

botched transparent face
that will never tan.
I'm an artefact, I know,

yet some kind of human –
I can think with halting fluency,
admire sunsets, want love. . .

At home, the mirror is edged
with cloud stains –
a *fin-de-siècle* lithograph.

Diving through deep-sea eyes
I ask, *How much is retrievable,
how much yet unborn?*

then turn away – terminally bemused,
of course, but also, I confess,
quickened, scenting an animal peace.

November Morning, Boston

'Nature,' said Monet, dismissing pointillism,
'is not composed of dots.'
                                   Today, dots
crowd the air, buoyant in the down-draught,
silhouette black trees, fill grooves and runnels
of bark; spiky bushes become nests for them.
Smoke from chimneys and grates sifts through them.
Our feet come to know new textures:
dough-clumps, sponge, crunchy dust.

Mouths open to receive them, or close
as if to exclude glass insects, lashes flutter
to prevent crisp teardrops stinging the eye.
Turning, they fall like dice – chance moving
in all directions. Earth harbours, consumes them.
After, air is a pure outline, a crystal breath.

CLOCK MUSEUM

Long-case clocks line ancient walls:
transformed trees; survivors proving time's
errant constancy. One strikes seven at four o'clock
with the certainty of tone that poets crave:
words dissolving in a sea of resonance.

Seismograph of oak; split Rorschach of walnut;
the honeyed shine of elm, crudely planed. . .
In leaf shapes, black traceries
track shadows over silver, point to
three straight cyphers that translate all hours.

Old clockmakers wished time to be
present to us, stand in drawing room or hall
breathing the air of our dramas – lofty yet
patient companions, benevolent totems,
whose faces can hold our gaze, take our measure.

The sombre ticking off of lives. . . As these
shapers of it knew, time works on weight –
gravitas of flesh and wood and metal,
all culled from earth to be embraced by light,
fall towards the darkness of new origins.

WINTER SOLSTICE, 1994

The moon is whole –
definitive inside a disc of haze
on starless indigo.

My lamp is its twin in the glass –
a halo of glued rice paper;
the globe of uncratered warmth

I write by. . . Down there,
a black swathe studded with
street lights, gold windows.

Eucalypts fork through them,
nest the sky:
horizons were made to be broken.

Night-gusts will sweep this city,
winnow what has been held in air,
(tingled on skin, in the eye's memory) –

cold darkness will erase
stories unfinished or untold
till they rise again

like steam from pavements,
unravel crippled determined roots,
press through grass and garbage.

Meanwhile the molten moon
drains and renews the world's waters,
rhythms of brain and blood.

Sun-fertilised, it is a cell
hooked to the wall of night.
I draw curtains but cannot

switch it off: the moon's
unanswerable,
dying and growing, light.

AT THE MELBOURNE GENERAL CEMETERY

Some interesting angels.
At this time of year, cowslips –
watery sculpture of lemon-meets-yellow.
Lichen-crested, old gravestones cluster
near untried slabs, grey scripted with gold.

I walk here to come back to myself. . .
Today, unhappy beyond knowing much else,
I am grounded by simple acts
of subtraction: contemplate again
how many children have died young;
those thirty-year widowhoods;
a life begun in Canton a long century ago.

There are a few light touches:
a guitar of paper blooms for Elvis,
red bordering white; in veinless marble,
the billiard balls and cue of Walter Lindrum.
Epitaphs graced by kitsch seem fair enough –
death the ultimate test of words.
And of flowers . . . lily, carnation, marigold
so rarely fresh here, except for those
heaped over the newly dead, or brought with
weekly care till the grave is re-opened.

A little fine rain is chastening enough –
I need not to be shriven by fear of endings,
or so I tell myself: with a childhood shadowed by
crucifixes, skulls stared at by mad saints. . .
By now I know death as states of suffering
not to be endured, yet endured:
black lakes and seas rowed over
are now a sediment layering the body.

Why blame death if I made a bad bargain with life?

Survivor and witness, I walk the often-turned earth
of this place where cypress and eucalypt
spring up as they can, or will,
against horizons of glass-skinned skyscrapers,
lobelia dream-folds of mountain.

The day's air a cool pressure
to be accepted or denied.

In Memory

HOME

When the time comes to die
there is a rightness in dying.

The surgeon who will not operate again,
the one you trust, affirms your decision

to leave the hospital, go home.
The other, who promised life,

of whatever kind, on half a liver,
snubs us as we walk by. He's known as

The Butcher. The lift speeds down past
Speech Pathology, Stomal Therapy,

the Department of Rehabilitation,
the Department of Resuscitation,

and you are out in sunlight again,
a free man, delivered from your dread

of hospitals. It's summery, you lean back,
shawled, in dark glasses, peaked cap,

tell me I drive well, knowing
I've come late to this maturity.

Then it's district nurses, physios,
pills and paraphernalia,

but mostly what is, is home. And us.

We will do what can be done
when nothing can be done.

You settle down to things, grateful,
uncertain: the last phase.

If death teaches us how to live,
the lives we have lived teach us how to die.

This is the harvest, and the cutting down.

MUSIC, POETRY

Music. Soul food
for one who cannot eat.

Not Beethoven's late quartets.
No. But much of Mozart,

and Boccherini, Pachelbel. . .
Towards the year's end

we hear *Enfance du Christ* –
human polyphonies,

spirals of grace, humility.
You speak as with surprise

of spending Christmas
with your family.

It's my brother who's musical,
tunes our energy

like an instrument,
chooses the moment.

Then my poems. I read the ones
whose titles you announce

as if etched into your brain,
which satisfy you

in some deep place,
while I register how tentative,

how cluttered, words are.
My brother spins out thoughts

on his guitar, notes drift
through unlit rooms and garden.

In both our inherited gifts
you take pleasure –

talents you could not live out –
a trunkful of stories burnt

in youth; hands that withdrew
from their own authority of touch

in playing Schumann, Schubert –
your best, you believed,

would not serve.
Hard physical labour

saw to the rest –
fifty years of exhaustion.

> There is the life we live
> and the life we do not live.
>
> In you those streams are
> reconciled, becoming one.

VIDEO

Even with death so close,
life must go on. Especially so.

We sit by you –
wife, daughter, son

who made up
your utterly private universe,

your solace – though families
are never pure solace.

Together we watch *Turtle Diary*,
follow the unromantic plot

to where the turtles
enter an unknown sea,

great bodies that can express
no trace of feeling or memory,

can only trundle towards
the tide edge, lift into lightness,

be absorbed by the amniotic fluid
that swathes the world.

After, reassured by that image,
you lapse back into solitude,

resting, dreaming.

STORIES

I sit on the bed beside you,
reading aloud. A ripple
of night coolness billows in.

Though you are close to death,
gently your hand rises to flick
an edge of sheet across my legs.

It's forty years since we have
sat on the same bed, engaged
in the reading of stories.

Long ago they were of king
and queen, and of their daughter
who eats the poisoned apple.

Though paralysed, as if by death,
for many years, she does
survive to tell the story.

We try detective fiction now:
mazes brutal and excruciating
around the mystery of death.

But – coffee grounds, fag ends:
the style somewhat disappoints,
we're not compelled. . .

You gather yourself into sleep,
transparently,
as I fall silent.

MINISTRATION

Over the silhouettes
of crimson trees

into gulfs
partly inaccessible

taking sparse outcrops
with a tentative blade

then round the solid line
of chin, unwrinkling

folds beside the mouth. . .
Constantly checking

my perspective,
I work with

intimate distance.
At the end,

'A good shave,' you say
in your old dry way,

bony hand stretching
smooth skin –

a satisfied customer.
With an artist's

flair I slap on
the aftershave.

DYING

It seemed you were dying back then.
I remember your saying – cheekbones
rising from whiteness, frame three stone
lighter – 'I would like to feel the sun
upon my face . . . to have a few more years.'

Today, sickle-leaf wings in summer air.
At the window, a fall of light patterns
my wrist with bronze wires. My hair,
red at birth, is now grey. Yours
I can recall jet black, though it has long been

white. Seven years you were given
to close your circle of life. Within
a fading room, you unseal the resolution
of your lips: 'The wheel must turn';
gaze at sunlight through half-drawn curtains.

PAIN

Promises of a painless death with the drugs.
Close to the end, the doctor predicts
you'll 'just drift quietly away,' your coma
'an almost pleasant experience.' None of it true,
and besides, you have fought your way back,
opening partly filmed eyes wide in the grey air;
you have last business, farewells to make;
slowly, you look round at each of us.

Then, a stay in time. By turns we wander
into your room to sit with you, do this
and that, or leave you in rest, glancing back
from the doorway. Now the final coma:
your eyes will not open again to this world,
greet these shadowy familiar faces with surprise.

DEATH

(i)

We, your children, were there
in other rooms

and my mother beside you;
yet you died

without witnesses. . .
Was that how you wished it,

death's ultimate privacy?
So clear and frail you lay

jaw set in closure,
the drama consummated.

I was the one who'd known
inside my bones

how far from death,
and when you would go.

But, guiltily tired,
I kept no vigil,

was called from dreams
by my brother. All of us

kept watch for a while,
slept again.

(ii)

Long ago.
You'd let me sleep,

an exhausted eight-year-old,
rather than take myself to mass.

Unversed in mortal sin,
you'd calmed my sorrow

saying, 'God will understand' –
unwaveringly, as if you knew.

Once only did you use that word,
eschewing fixities

though prey to restless doubt.
Later, you'd ask

did I ever wonder
what it was all about,

your mind working at
puzzles, painful memories.

You anchored yourself
in what you had learnt,

the knowledge of what you must do.
Out of innocence,

a quietly difficult life,
you shaped a wisdom

and inherit the reward of seeking:
the gift of a good death.

HERE

On the day after you died
my mother heard your voice
call her name;

sitting in the garden
I felt, for the first time
in my life, tranquillity.

By the fifth day
we had begun to know you
as an absence,

exhaustion catching us
as we moved
backwards towards

subtle amnesias,
more startled
rememberings.

That afternoon in the garden
told me there are no
questions or answers,

presences or absences,
that there is no
death or life.

Who you were, or are,
retains all its force
of mystery, father:

now a voice in the soul
I learn to know you
a little better.

DAY OF THE FUNERAL

Much essential knowledge comes later.

Today I learn camellias were your favourite flower,
you'd had a gift for cultivating them.

Here in your garden, a slight wind
makes its unobtrusive claim on us.

Far above, vast gatherings of birds
dissolve and resurrect their bodies' density,

shape patterns out of separateness,
infolded by a universe of air.

They cannot shadow us, or eclipse the mild sun.
In this cavern of roots and branches,

we are drawn into Memory
which codes itself inside heartbeat,

dwells in the spaces between us.

GRAVESIDE VISIT – I

Almost a year now. Over the months
we've returned to tend your grave,
set right the levelled tombstone,
unroll a carpet of grass that took,
grew lushly. Now summer-dry, it harbours
thistles, rabbit droppings. We clear these,
place fresh flowers, stand there briefly.

Where are you now? I imagine an ease
of understanding, any last anguishes
healed. I want to believe you fulfilled
in our memory of you. I take my mother's arm.
How the wind comes over the hill
as we walk away, hearing the sea beyond
the cypresses, the voices of summer's children.

GRAVESIDE VISIT – II

Spring warmth, fatigue
  air stretching itself
    pressuring skin, earth
      reshaping trees
        the hair of our heads
        as we bend to snip grass
      coax out weeds
    stapled to dry soil:
swift powdery exits.

To be buried on a hill
  by the sea, in an old
    disorganised cemetery:
      graves marble-majestic
      or simple like this –
      uneven turf, wild violets.
    My mother puts azaleas,
  cinerarias, white daisies
impacted with yellow galaxies

beneath the headstone
  with space left for her name.
    Freesias star the hill,
      light billows over us,
        clouds ferry a burning white.
      Under them, the sea:
    flat indeterminate jewel;
  a vastness of small movements
towards, away from.

GRAVESIDE VISIT – III

Beyond pain, but not beyond knowledge,

you dwell beneath and above cineraria,
white rose, camellia. We trim the grass

with shears, (flesh-grass with time's shears),
pluck out the star-shaped weed

cradling a crystal drop. Walking away,
my mother does not need my arm

so much as in the first two years,
but it's companionable like this.

We drive to the Heads where we'll tread
sand, contemplate a strait of blue light

linking, severing.

LITTORAL

After the solstice,
expansions, slow blossomings;
light prising apart the edges

of each day. Coral over blue,
a reef of cloud dissolves in this
shining margin hollowed by footprints.

You walked here with my mother
when the sea air was mild,
knew peace from the shared years.

The shore sweeps away from headland
to lighthouse, from the town
you lived in to where you were buried.

At the last, what held you in life
was a stubborn integrity,
the desire to die well.

Not for you the singular radiance
of extreme old age, or its risk:
consciousness adrift, or partly drowned.

A half century of killing work,
prolonged suffering of mind and flesh:
your timing was right, perhaps,

able to leave us in the spirit
in which you'd lived: subtly humorous,
gently present, your stoicism

a husk round a core of acceptance;
throughout all, a wish never to impose,
though there were glimpses of rage.

For each of us a setting free from fear,
your words and silences becoming
seeds in time; taking root in memory.

Sites

Homecomings

IN TRANSIT

Through an egg-shaped eye,
lid pulled half down,
I track long level snowfields.

Sudden openings –
a blue ravine, river, or lake,
their deepest depth
the ocean's surface.

Whiteness blows past,
I glimpse a thinner blue
above, lit by sunburst.

Now the lid is closed,
I sit inside dimness where
a single focused light
determines this page.

FAMILY SOJOURN

(i) Jet Lag, Fever

Bored with my small dark room
I bring my fever out into the sun –
fighting heat with heat. In dressing gown,
sunglasses, slung in fold-up chair,
I watch starlings in a shimmer of
bronze and ebony. A far gull stitches
pines and eucalypts together.
Everywhere, a crimson or green
translucency as my father and mother
weed, re-arrange, tend future life.
A magpie opens its beak's red chamber,
yawns; swooping low over this
floral runway, it leaves to inhabit
some other part of the afternoon.

(ii) Kaleidoscope

To Kyle, my nephew

Inside your new kaleidoscope you place
fern leaf, petal, moonstone earring.
We lie on the lounge room floor,
angle it towards window and lampshade,
gasp at that jewelled flowering world.
Later, you giddily act out how planet earth
revolves around the sun, then wait to be
programmed, wearing a robot's silver smile.

Worlds we inherit, the worlds we invent. . .
Somewhere between the two we live,
gaze at the lit circle of feldspar, flower
and fern, in multiplied transparency –
cosmologies we may summon and dismiss
in an instant, or ponder in stillness.

The Journey Back

(i) Stopoff

This drop, once rain,
grows into what it holds –
curves towards sharpness,
trembles towards stillness.

So many imaginings
from such small slow drops! –
green fingers, amber phalli,
nose of ice-witch.

Under the neon glare, I long
for candlelight to infuse
this deep space, touch
each falsely translucent drop. . .

In warm dusk, rising winds
stir the leaves of eucalypts,
the first star seeps through
a cavern of sapphire-blue, glints.

(ii) Night Driving

Two speeding beams
inside night's enormity.
You concentrate, refusing
dreams, siren-fantasies,
holding this moment and
the completed journey
in one thought. You pass
salt lakes, marshlands,
the sea-line's whispering
crash. The wind ripples
hillsides, changing one
green to another – somewhere
out there, all around you.
Tyres on stones, headlamps
startling eyes drugged
by so much darkness.
It is as though you are
pulled by a thread over
hundreds of miles,
making your small mark
in the dust, in the dew,
going back to where,
using the car lights as
a torch, you will fumble
with keys, then re-enter
memories, absences,
giving thanks,
the house totally lit up
before dawn comes.

VISITATION

Before sleep had ended, somewhere
an insistent tap dripping drops of lead.
But the waking house was soundless.
Then the glimpse of a bird hovering
in the half-light, pecking again
and again at that insoluble wall. . .

Often, soon after dawn it comes –
tenacious yellow beak, imprint of wings,
marking the dusty pane. Sharp eyes
pinion me: we are mysteries behind glass
to each other, trying to break through
transparency, discover new spaces
wherein to fly, to nest, to sing.

DUST

I am not afraid to live in this house,
this body, dream of its darkened rooms,
accustomed now to the sounds of structures
shifting a little deeper into earth.

As each day enters, I open curtains,
windows. Dust falls on my hand
moving across the sill to wipe it away,
that hand a higher form of dust
on which light also catches, is held.

GARDEN

Sticky clumps, dead insects, in my hair. . .
A spider has stencilled its kingdom
across the path to the water tank.
Next day my nose stops, inches from a bee
grappling its chains with strong black legs,
swaddled in musty filaments. I fail
to free it but damage the web again –
a message to build elsewhere.

Mid-afternoon, bees harvest blue
of the rosemary, the mint I tread gives up
its scent to me, to these warm shadows.

PEACH TREE

Late autumn. I watch light purify
while clouds grow heavier,
freighted with gold, cyclamen.

Vines have turned this tree
into a nest; tendrils snake
around boughs, thicken,
sprout more pointed tongues.

Resolutely, I unbind,
cut double, triple, sinews
and unresolvable soft knots.

Spade-shaped leaves fall
to reveal silver-brown bark,
a winter integrity.

I work downwards, wrest
multiple roots from
a woven floor, cease only
when all efforts fail,

knowing the vine will return
in its own time with renewed
strength to challenge mine.

SILENCE

Words fall away:
you listen to the silence
as it listens to you,
invites a beginning.
You summon your familiars –
a garden of sparrows
pecking at seeds, in disarray
beside the sprinkler;
chevrons of swans
crossing the sun; blink at
the flick flick of gulls
as the peach tree's shadow
lengthens to where you sit
behind glass doors. . .

What will be woven, made?
Your eyes search back
to touch new images,
gaze out at unhurried
green life, dew and
shadows under the sun.

SEASCAPE

Low tides drain peninsulas of rock,
billowing green islands. You walk past
depths you swam in last summer,
stir pools of kelp inlaid with marble:
you cull a baby's tooth, a crocodile tear.
Along the shore, weightless mounds
of seaweed give out the morning's heat –
sweet salty breath.
                           Sculptured by
water, stone plateaus unnerve
bare feet, the cliff you climb blown
slowly towards, lapsing away from,
this jewelled ocean. From the cliff top,
a view of sunken continents, skies
flecked with foam, a midday moon.

SUMMER'S END

No dolphins that night. The estuary
around me then falling away as I stepped
in a skin of light to witness
clouds from a furnace-heart, the sun
a meteorite in slow motion, then
bubble of mercury on phosphorus.

The child's hand placed absently,
trustingly, on my thigh for a long minute
as we stood in half-dream till his mother
claimed him with laughter, the boy too small
for embarrassment, the sun a meniscus
but plotting fireworks after its drowning,
to tell us with triumph, as heat turns
to silence, that summer is over.

In the Blue Mountains

AT WENTWORTH FALLS

A waterfall of rock splits open the mountain;
steppes and gulfs dyed rust, titian.
In a tangle of ropes, streams plummet
to form a seamless skin. I break rods
of platinum as they plunge into crystal,
wade over hard ripples with toes curled.
From the cascade a smoky rain blows up:
skin swathed by tingling dampness.

Rainbows of spray; pools in hollowed
hands of stone abandoned by sun. Dusk
gathers and amplifies light, as rock, water.
Memories glide over leaves: faded
gold petals, slow butterflies dancing.
I climb the fluid permanence of stone.

RAIN

At Wentworth Falls

Suddenly there beyond the drop of trees:
a dense grey masking skylines of rock,
that red figure on the valley floor.
Clay trickles towards me; I climb
casually, as if in clear weather,
past the couple under shelter, hear
the watery echo of my steps behind me,
my skirt bunched against drenching.

From inside this car, the rain is
a cool noise healing the mountain's
dryness before summer. My hair drips
on the page as I write – becoming
misted in until I turn the key, drive
with an open window past drowning vistas.

Rainforest Walk

At Witches' Leap Falls, Katoomba

Two ants manoeuvre a moth down
earthen steps – a wildly acrobatic team
leaping round blades, webbed shoots.
I move more slowly in the scale of things,
stop often to breathe or finger globes
of the rice flower, curled downy promise
of fern beside its unfurled symmetry –
cool reassurance between open palms.

Across the gorge, a white zigzag
through silver. . . Eyes waver, centre on
stillness again: powdery moss,
rock filmed by drops from the falls.
Back in sunlight, I watch cicadas stagger,
their hymn a keening inside the ear.

Rainforest Ferns

Leaves of the coral fern: knotty conundrums
that straighten to lines of dot matrix.
Intricate as a rune, a tree fern's infolded
wings inside their bronze membrane.
Everywhere, bishop's crooks, scrolls,
through the cathedral-dim forest.
Enmeshed in lushness, or held by survival's
thread, they unfurl on tides of air.

Along the rockface, ferns trace the curve
of vanished seas. I peer upwards
as a drop falls, then a leaf. In decay,
copper discs harden, mocha invades lime.
Mature ferns hover in their long moment,
luminously fresh, starred with twilight.

AFTER RAIN

In sight of Katoomba Falls

Each tree and bush a galaxy as the falls
plummet with a vengeance, strike
sparks from the escarpment. Streams
cup boulders, swerve through undergrowth.
New leaves crowd grottos untouched by rain
as if, lacking gales or spiral gusts,
to live in that moist air were enough.

Drops dampen my hair, cool my skin,
as I remember the falls split between
day and dusk, mauve or emerald veiling
ferns on a flooded ledge. In the wind,
crimson and cobalt billowed out across
dry rock till dark closed over, that weight
of water arrowing towards a dank silence.

WATERFALL

You crouch on a template of wet stone.
Quicksilver tongues leap from a silken drop
that spreads to embrace this plateau,
work hairline fractures to gulfs,
unlock earth from bare tree roots.
From sky-filled rocks, the stream hurtles,
erratic needle of light, towards the valley.

You crouch and listen, your fingers
touch the water's pulse, its flight
from source to turbulent birthing.
Near your hand, a splashed leaf –
pearls in a green ear. Rhythms of spray
ghost that line of crystal, envelop
its voice with a soundless singing.

NEAR KATOOMBA FALLS

Today, your mind closed in,
only the steps before you sinking down
to the rainforest. Mist floods the valley,
curlicues rise to uncoil in freer air.
The leaves you tread are copper, oxblood,
wear a leathery sheen after the rain.

Clumps of moss are forests in miniature
grounded, like this one, on rock: from ledges,
eucalypts struggle towards grey light;
coach trees stretched thinly upwards
sway with each lift of wind. Deadlocked
in space, roots arch and coil through paths.
An abseiler enters that eye in the cliff
to crouch inside the emptiness of stone.

At Jerrikellimi Cave *

The wind gusts then eases as we enter
an interval in stone, find sleeping place,
hearth, leaf through the visitors' book.
Outside, drops ricochet from basalt –
fireflies in a shaft of sunlight;
the billy ripples a pool clear as air.
Under the cobwebbed dome, we gaze at
tree-dense valley, slopes cupping blue cloud.

Stories are swapped, tea drunk,
while time measures us with different eyes.
We ascend with footholds on roots,
hands steadied by saplings. Almost there
we rest, among unknown birdcalls,
at home on the mountain.

* Named and used as a holiday place by Eleanor
  and Eric Dark and their children.

Mountain Scene

Cars, pulsating bodies, fill the track
nudge the solitary walker towards wet grass.
Shouted names, thick muscles on turf
as a silent whiteness blows in,
the whole oval disappearing under
arc lights: alien eyes that do not see.
Whistles blow, a commanding voice pierces
the wall of air, as cars sidle away,
intrude stark haloes between trees.

Climb the path, step back into stillness
where the currawong swerved into grace
through clear dusk air. A space around you
then scrub in the trammels of teasing smoke
that moves in relation, an enfolding distance.

GARDENS

At Mount Wilson

Scarcely any wind to shake the blooms.
Everywhere, the crimson and tangerine
and mauve of azalea or rhododendron.
The sequoia cannot be seen whole –
an epic beside their brief resonance,
stored with a century of sun and shadow.
In the late afternoon, these are one;
you stroll beneath wisteria to a perfect
white gazebo. But it is the garden
which looks in at you, calls you out again
to almost touch crinkled bubbles
of pink, rim the first decay on cream,
smell those barely-orange flowers,
unnameable, in mountain air.

At Hawthornden Castle

FIRST WALK

Sooner or later, the world comes
to meet you: as the keep gate opens,
green turns to white – the verge
a train of seed-pearls in early sun.

On the drive you are back in dusk,
tree shapes striping the gravel;
then the road where warmth
has a purchase on the day,
your breath no longer a tease
of vapour.
          Glass bubbles bend
grass tips; crows slice air
with serrated wings, voices.

BIRCH

Always the driven, frustrated
maker, I remember
shantungs I sewed when
young, the oil paints
I failed to teach myself
to use: half-mixed tints
drenching the blond wood.

Slubbed and burnished,
this trunk is stained
the colours of tea and rose hips,
amber, linseed oil, rust.
Flies feast on the green
eroding its silver.

Here, at the drive's turn,
all decay and triumph,
this tree draws hand and eye
more strongly than any other.

BUDS

A reddishness
        like a faint hum
                in far trees.
Close up, spurs
        sheathed in
                bronze silk;
others are suavely
        gloved claws,
                breasts cupped by
brocade – in black,
        musky cyclamen,
                milk-green.
Soon, frothy handkerchiefs
        will drop
                as from a wrist,
chrysolite beads
        as from an ear,
                the shape of buds
no longer
        a layered smoothness
                in your mouth
as they answer back
        with scalloped
                edges of softness.
Then the valley
        studded with
                tiny antennae
will become
        a sea of
                chameleon green –
with mists
        and waterfalls
                and bowers of it
deepening
        inside your eye.

BUMBLE BEE

Revealing the unity
of all things,

touching a daffodil here,
a forget-me-not there,

lost in a rabbit hole
then zooming from blade to tree top –

a bird/beast,
weightless and hairily cumbersome,

a carpeted feather
struggling to ride on air,

forge out a fresh route
to the desired.

From pause to pause
it moves like thought,

the appraised left quickly
for the pristine,

with sudden aerial swerves
or close-to-the-ground

surveillance of detail. . .
Attired in the sumptuous

discretion of velvet,
it alights from nothingness

to gather tiny fruits of knowledge –
busy and meditative,

its voice a soft black hum
banded with gold.

CLOCK

The dining room clock picks its teeth
　　　　as we eat. Above our talk of poetry
　　　　　　　it chants, *Ink blot! Ink blot!*

Huge as a railway station dial, it snipes,
　　　　Be worried. It's almost too late.
　　　　　　　How can you just sit there?

Defiantly, we raise glasses to lips which sip
　　　　the present moment again and again,
　　　　　　　insist that time well passed

lives in later time. When the hour chimes,
　　　　that silver echo holds through
　　　　　　　twenty seconds. The tick is

one large drop, one small, falling from
　　　　branch to lily pond. I see a woman
　　　　　　　with a limp climbing stairs –

a persistence inside the wavering,
　　　　her mind poised between each
　　　　　　　new step and the last.

The clock face is cracked enamel,
　　　　smoke-blackened by a century.
　　　　　　　It knows what is unsaid,

listens to the sound of itself thinking.
　　　　Sometimes, silences before it
　　　　　　　remembers to beat –

heart-pauses,
　　　　a circumspection before
　　　　　　　the fact of time.

Venice Notebook

1

At first you want to restore each façade,
remove each trace of centuries-old dirt,
modern acid – all to please your eye.

Next morning, a river of light bathes
wounds in crimson plaster; a sparrow
perches among ancient geraniums.

You open windows, breathe – you are here.

2

From a balcony, greenery grows down
towards a white sheet edged with heavy lace,
and another, sky-blue with swirls of cloud;
both are of vast proportions.

Behind glass, an interior gleams
with cameos, figurines, spring flowers –
life flourishing in miniature,
with scope enough for grand gestures.

3

The water's glitter
makes its way up walls,
a ghostly creeper,

moving inside your
room, over the ceiling,
down your arms

as you sit writing.
Once, music floats
over a sill crowded

with tulips. You hear
Vivaldi swallow-weaving
Venetian light, imagine

that light flowing
over him as he sits,
dreaming, inscribing.

4

With people, I only glance, stroll past;
but with cats, pigeons, and masks,
I am studious.
                    The pigeons see all,
see nothing, mesmerised by a dream
of showers of corn.
                    Cats give back
stare for stare, too insolent
to take offence.
                    And the masks
are watching before I stop at
their windows, or as I walk away –
not looking back, unsnubbable.

5

Pigeons live in crevices, behind gargoyles –
they live everywhere. Today, thronging in
the square, they form a collective of
bright-eyed indifference. Suddenly
the air is fanned by their wings,
hundreds are following an old man
to his door. Soon he stands among them,
flinging seeds from a paper bag. They are
his disciples; layered wing on wing, they feed
                    on his smallest words.

6

The mask-maker stands in the dusk
at the back of his shop, hunched over
a sun which radiates from his hands;
its gilded rays frame a too-cheerful grin.
On the bench, a new moon smiles softly.

At Carnival, you become what you are not,
or what you are – some secret self.
But who will assume this old woman's
face with its maze of wrinkles
and Medusa-tangle of white hair?
Centering the display, it is surrounded
by Scorpion, Double Face, Jolly Old Man.

7

From her verandah, my neighbour
starts arguments with passers-by,
lifts agèd hands in greeting.

Above the canal's grey sheen,
light etches her face more deeply
each day. No need to tell her

the great river is always moving on. . .
Witch-like, she contemplates
mist, falling away or rising;

geraniums, shrivelling or blazing;
hears cat fights, the play
of children, songbirds in cages.

8

Along cobbles by the canal,
young girls are playing late,
will come to no harm.

Their laughter punctuates words
I am beginning, at last,
to recognise:
      domani, luna, stupido.

When Carla's mother calls
down to her, the sound is
a shimmering orange scarf

unfurled in the night air,
hovering.

9

As the island becomes
a familiar labyrinth

you uproot yourself,
probe *vicolo*, cul-de-sac,

till you light on a hotel
known six years before

in another existence
you do not want to remember.

Clean, anonymous, austere,
it is eminently erasable.

You turn tail, head for the water.

10

As if it were a bar, young men
smoke, stub their butts
in the portico of Saint Mark's.

Among fanta cans, film boxes,
I stare out from the gallery
to where a girl spits at her lover
in the centre of the Square.

They argue till wordless
inside a space filled with
pigeons and schoolchildren,
corn sellers, spivs. . .

Lenses close in on pearl-
pink walls, forked shadows,
the lagoon at midday
a mosaic of gold leaf.

11

One doorway leads in to another.
Baroque saints, fresh flowers,
votary candles askew, as if
pulled by different winds.

Crimson drapes frame the altar's
drama, ornate boxes set high.
With roof-windows open,
the church is preserving itself.

You are here to light candles again,
ask for modest, essential things:
good heart, common sense,
a measure of hope.

But this is the land of opera!
Why don't you ask for something
extravagant, like an unselfish
lover, or one moment –

only one – when you stand,
alive to every petal and shadow,
your hand a glitter of dust motes
in stained glass air.

12

It would be good to have a painter
who knew everything about red –
          how it lies hidden in rust and gold,
          holds multiplicities of rose. . .

It would be good to have a painter
who knew that red never really goes away:
          first bud of spring; last leaf of autumn;
          winter-hard berry; summery hibiscus. . .

So shall I toast you, Titian,
in burgundy, claret, or rosé?

Now I am opening this peach-tinted grappa
which I should not have bought,
should not be drinking. . .

I raise a small measure
into the light that follows sunset.
Interesting! *Salute!*

13

On the one morning I am hungover
the police call. They want to know
when and where and why and what.

I offer dates, hypotheses,
false regrets for unsigned forms.
They juggle notebooks, words...

Fortunately, two half-languages
do not make a whole... A far cry
from inquisitive forbears,

they wear broad gold bands,
sport avuncular bellies. Concerned,
one points to my bare feet on marble.

The final week... Saturnine eyeballs
confer. What to do but shrug,
set shadowed jaws, leave?

14

The church is a maze of altars and angles
at any time, but today, Holy Saturday,
a mammoth Christ-on-the-Cross
slants through reshuffled pews.
Against the cavernous dark,
candles, electric and real.

With even his dog at a loss,
a blind man stumbles, displaces
a woman in black. Decades of piety
have not prepared her for this: she sidles
away, unable to find the gesture. The squat
priest bends at his shoulder, offers words' solidity.

15

Matteo's *nonna* wheels his pram over
cobbles, bundles it over bridges,
singing his name and shouting:
'*Piccolo bello! Piccolo bello!*'

Matteo's almost transparent lids
are closing: now he no longer hears her
but has begun to dream her voice. . .
Hard work, being a baby in Italy.

16

Today, the peace summit.
In a gilded room, the President
talks and smiles beneath unseen
cobwebs woven by very old spiders. . .

His face to the sea, a monk
in saffron robes, white shirt,
prays for peace on the Zattere.
His figured drum beats
soft-soft-loud-soft-loud.

A roar in ripples, a well-aimed splash
flushed triumph behind a wheel. . .

Slowly, the monk gathers his things,
shifts ground, resumes his chant.

The sun is beginning to set.
People stroll past his back,
look out at gold light, gold water.